'Going to the mountains is going home.'

John Muir
Born Dunbar Scotland 21 April 1838

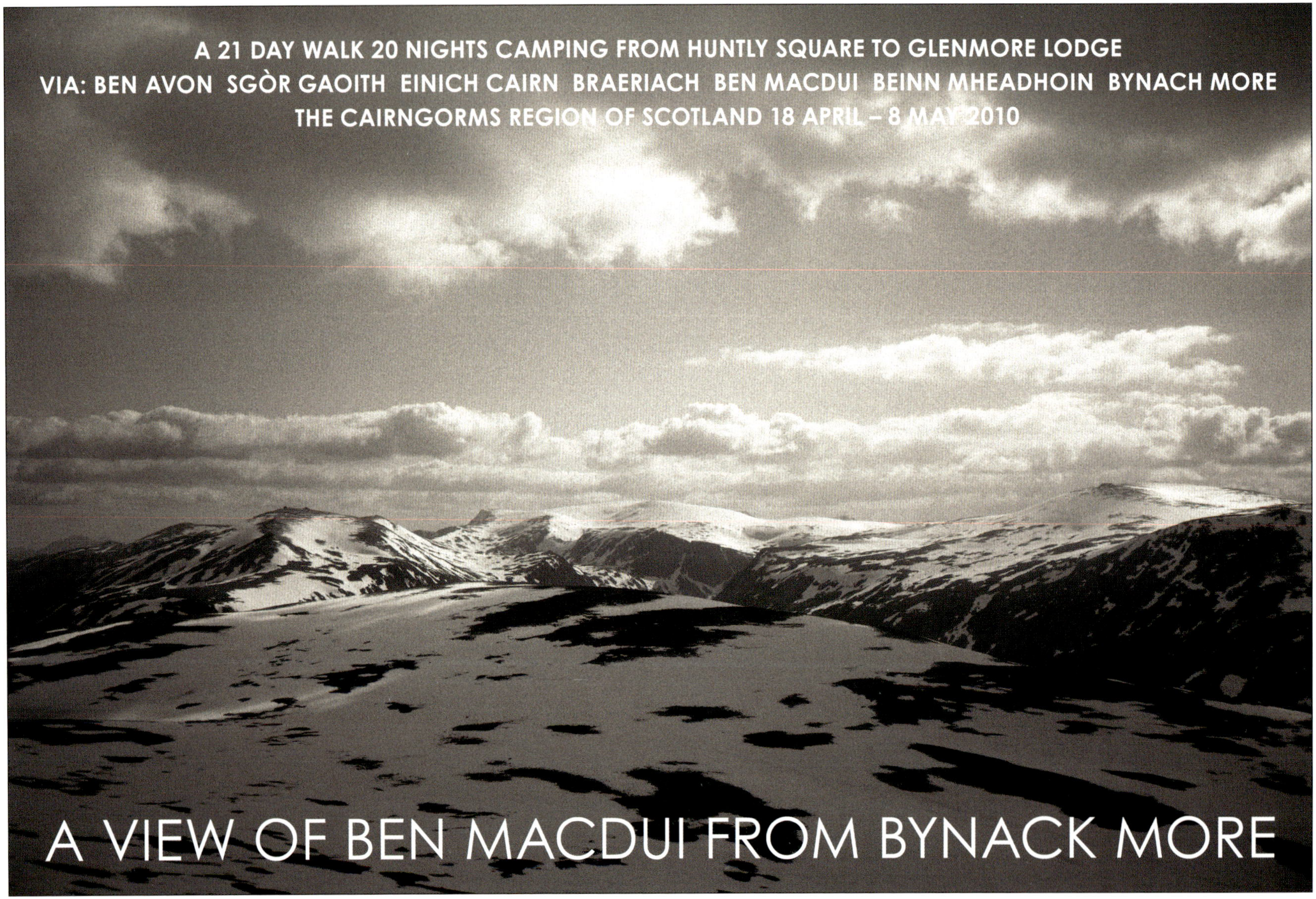
A 21 DAY WALK 20 NIGHTS CAMPING FROM HUNTLY SQUARE TO GLENMORE LODGE
VIA: BEN AVON SGÒR GAOITH EINICH CAIRN BRAERIACH BEN MACDUI BEINN MHEADHOIN BYNACH MORE
THE CAIRNGORMS REGION OF SCOTLAND 18 APRIL – 8 MAY 2010
A VIEW OF BEN MACDUI FROM BYNACK MORE

MOUNTAIN TIME
HUMAN TIME

CHARTA

HAMISH FULTON

HAMISH FULTON—21 DAYS IN THE CAIRNGORMS

Deveron Arts is based in Huntly in Aberdeenshire. It has no gallery or arts centre. Instead, the 'town is the venue' is its leitmotif. As such, it arranges projects that take place in existing spaces and within the surrounding landscape. The boundaries for the Cairngorms, as with other national parks, are often debated. They are defined through a combination of landscape features, political requirements and more practical reasons. As a result, some communities fall within the boundaries and others stay outwith. Some communities who are out would prefer to be in, to benefit from tourism and other advantages the park may bring. Others who are inside have to handle the drawbacks, like building restrictions and expensive housing. While we may be situated well outside the park, spiritual and economic links—and a soft spot for walking—link us to the Cairngorms.

Hamish Fulton sums up his work in a simple statement of intent: 'No walk, no work'. Only the texts and photographs allow us to engage with his experience. 'All walking is good', says Hamish. 'There is no one sort of walking better than another': short walking, long walking, walking for leisure or walking for personal endurance, walking for protest. Hamish Fulton has walked from one end of the British Isles to the other, climbed Mt Everest, made long-distance walks in Alaska, Spain and many other places, joined protest walks for Tibet, arranged many choreographed walks, and strolled around Canterbury's even landscape. And now Hamish has been roaming for 21 days around the Cairngorms with one rucksack only.

He started his *21 Days in the Cairngorms* right on the Square in the centre of our market town. On the first day he was accompanied by some thirty locals on his way to the national park boundaries, walking over Clashmach Hill, through the glens of Tillathrowie and Coynachie into the depopulated Cabrach that links seamlessly into the park.

On the day before he left Huntly, Hamish choreographed a walk around a block of buildings, instructing us all to walk exactly two metres behind each other for two full hours without altering our pace. Three weeks later—with no shops, no B and Bs, just Hamish himself, his rucksack and tent in one of the last wildernesses in Europe—on arrival at Glenmore Lodge in the heart of the Cairngorms, we joined in another choreographed walk staged in a semicircle, challenged to walk three metres forward for one hour.

What all these walks have in common—whether they are short or long, for a purpose or mere leisure, within or without arbitrary boundaries—is the notion of meditation, of being able to think differently through the rhythms of our feet. For us, Huntly's motto 'Room to Roam', with its geographic link to the wilds of the Cairngorms and its national park, was opened up both physically and spiritually.

Claudia Zeiske
Deveron Arts

MOUNTAIN TIME

A 21 DAY WALK 20 NIGHTS CAMPING

1 2 3 4 5 6 7 8 9 10 11 12

FROM HUNTLY SQUARE TO GLENMORE LODGE

HUMAN TIME

VIA: BEN AVON SGÒR GAOITH EINICH CAIRN BRAERIACH BEN MACDUI BEINN MHEADHOIN BYNACH MORE

13 14 15 16 17 18 19 20 21

THE CAIRNGORMS REGION OF SCOTLAND 18 APRIL – 8 MAY 2010

RESPECT THE MOUNTAIN RESPECT THE RIVER

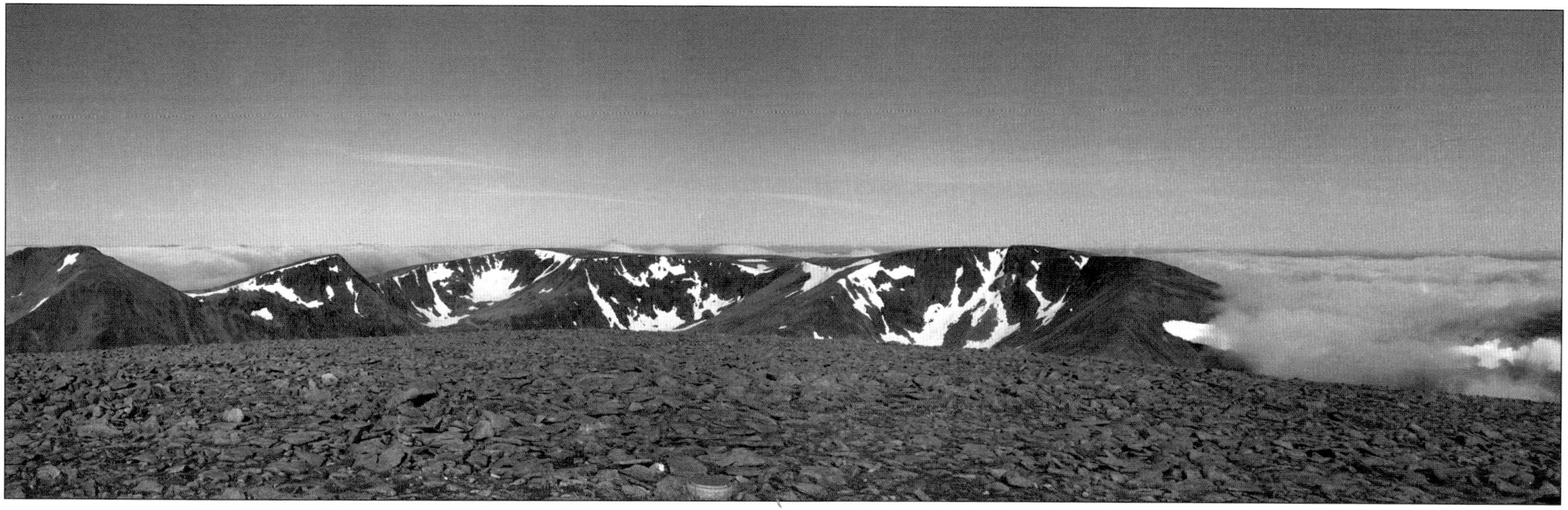

A WALK FROM THE SUMMIT OF BEN NEVIS TO THE SUMMIT OF BEN MACDUI BY WAY OF LOCH ERICHT SCOTLAND 18 19 20 21 JUNE 1975

W A L K I N G

1 2 3 4 5 6 7

A SEVEN DAY WANDERING WALK EIGHT NIGHTS CAMPING
STARTING ON THE DAY OF THE MAY FULL MOON CAIRNGORMS SCOTLAND 1999

Rothiemurchus
Creag an Leth-Choin
Lochan Buidhe
Ben Macdui
Loch Etchachan

Beinn Mheadhoin
Coire Etchachan
Glas Alte Mor
Moine Bhealaidh
Coire Ruairidh

Beinn A' Bhuird
Cnap a Chleirich
Leabaidh an Daimh Bhuidhe
Dubh Lochan
Carn Fiaclach
Allt an t-Sneachda
Dubh-Ghleann
Allt an Aghidh Mhilis
Lairig an Laoigh
Glen Derry
Glen Luibeg
River Dee
Glen Geusachan
Loch nan Stuirteag
Einich Cairn
Coire Bogha-cloiche
Allt a Choire Ghuirm
Lochan Odhar
Rothiemurchus
Allt an Lochain Odhair
Sron na Lairige
Braeriach
Einich Cairn
Allt Loch nan Cnapan
Sgor Gaoith
Sgoran Dubh Mor
Creag Dubh
Coire na Leacainn
Am Beanaidh
Rothiemurchus

CLIMATE

1 2 3 4 5 6 7

SEVEN DAYS WALKING SEVEN NIGHTS CAMPING IN A WOOD CAIRNGORMS SCOTLAND MARCH 1985

CHANGES

1 2 3 4 5 6 7

SEVEN DAYS WALKING SEVEN NIGHTS CAMPING CAIRNGORM MOUNTAINS SCOTLAND APRIL 2004

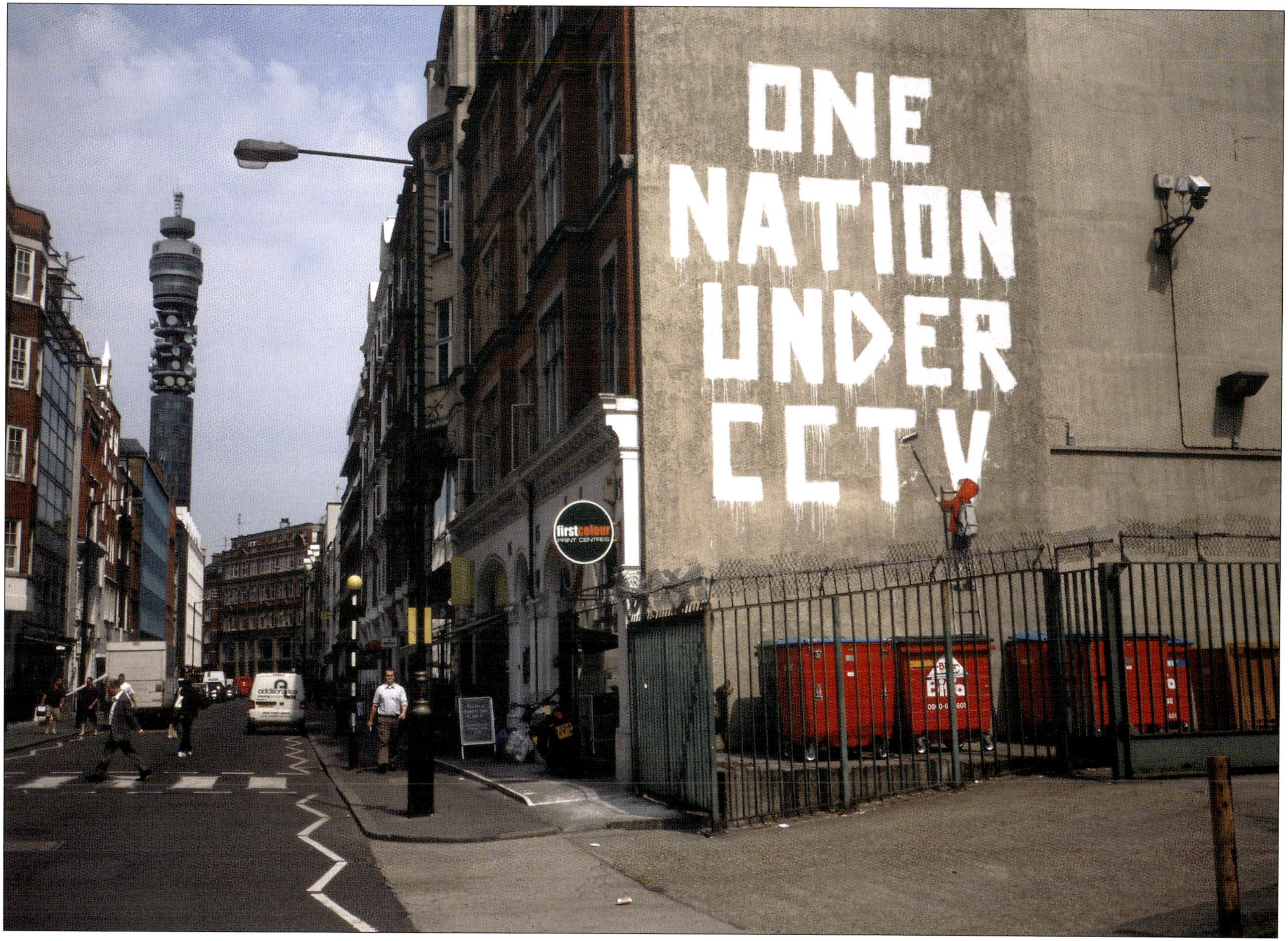

Graffiti by Banksy, London, 2008

Photo: Hamish Fulton

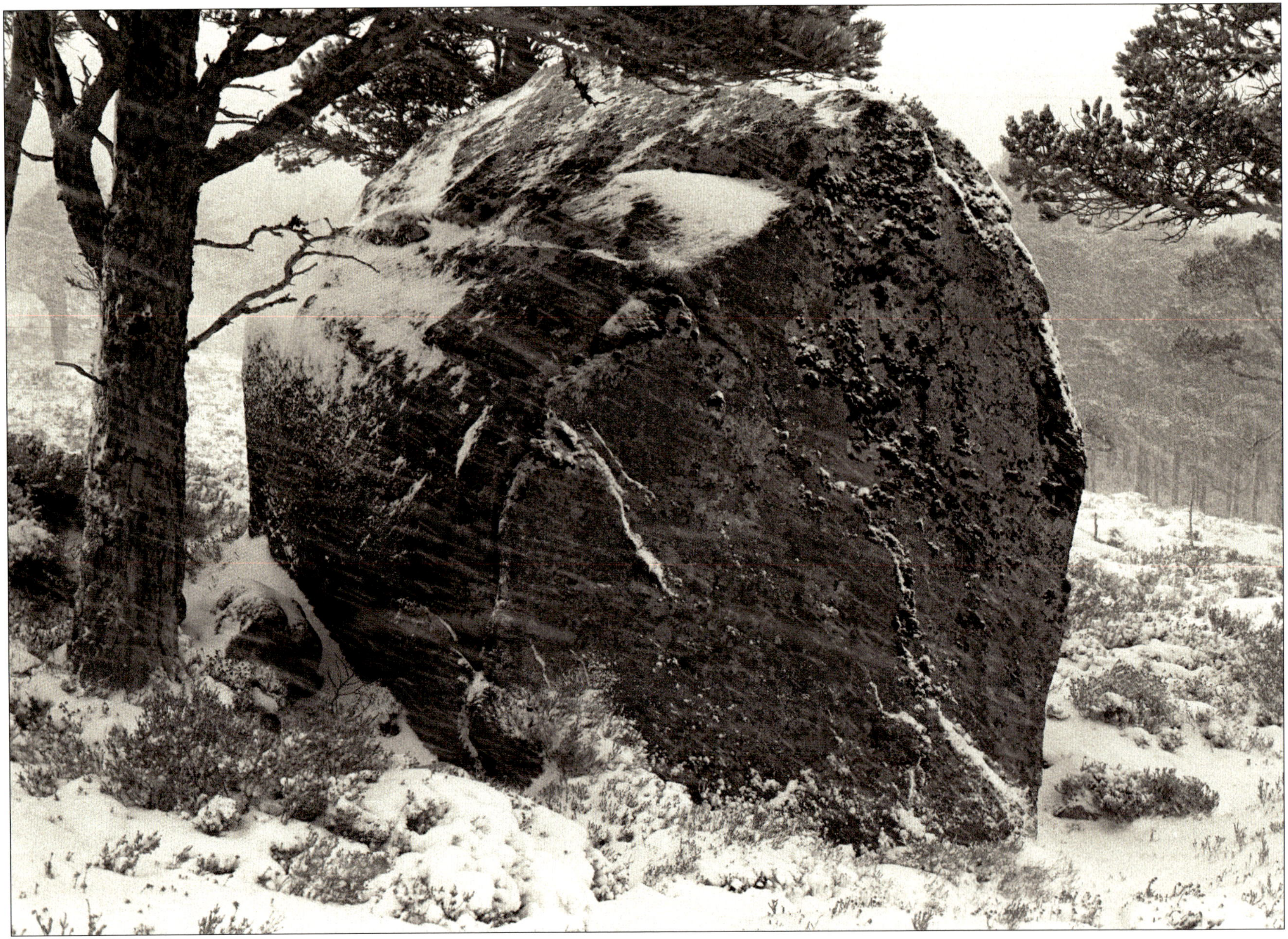

WALKING FOR SEVEN DAYS IN A WOOD CAIRNGORMS SCOTLAND JANUARY FULL MOON 1993

A TREE AT ITS BIRTHPLACE A BOULDER AT ITS RESTING PLACE

"I am going to venture that the man who sat on the ground in his tipi meditating on life and its meaning, accepting the kinship of all creatures, and acknowledging unity with the universe of things was infusing into his being the true essence of civilisation. And when native man left off this form of development his humanisation was retarded in growth."
—Luther Standing Bear, *Land of the Spotted Eagle*, 1933
(see p. 31)

"Because technology is now everywhere apparent, pervasive and obvious, we lose awareness of its presence. While we walk on pavements, or drive on a freeway, or sit in a shopping mall, we are unaware that we are enveloped by a technological and commercial reality, or that we are moving at technological speed. We live our lives in reconstructed, human-created environments; we are *inside* manufactured goods."
—Jerry Mander, *In the Absence of the Sacred*, 1991

"In Wildness is the preservation of the World."
—Henry David Thoreau, *Walking*, 1862
(see p. 61)

"Do people have ethical obligations towards rocks?
...To almost all Americans, still saturated with ideas historically dominant in Christianity... the question makes no sense at all. If the time comes when to any considerable group of us such a question is no longer ridiculous, we may be on the verge of a change of value structures that will make possible measures to cope with the growing ecologic crisis."
—Lynn White, Jr., *The Historical Root of Our Ecological Crisis* 1973
(see p. 18, 19)

"...rocks and mountains, sand, clouds, wind and rain... nothing is dead."
—Michael J. Cohen, *Prejudice Against Nature*, 1983
(see p. 22, 23)

"Since time is one of several luxuries that indigenous peoples enjoy more readily than we do, communications are characterised by deliberate slowness."
—Jerry Mander, *In the Absence of the Sacred*, 1991
(see p. 56)

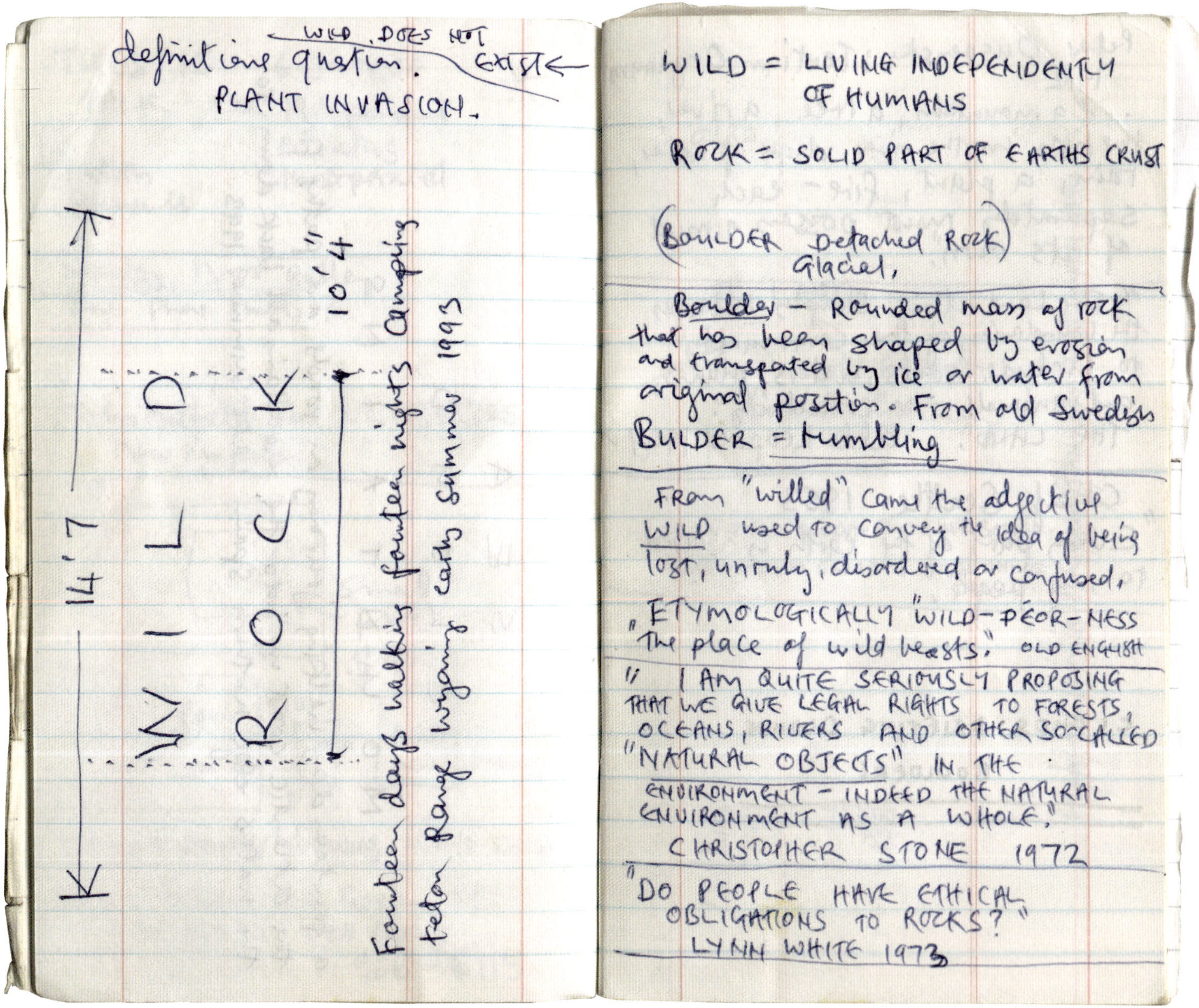

definitione question. WILD DOES NOT EXIST
PLANT INVASION.

14'7
WILD
ROCK
10'4"
Fourteen days walking fourteen nights camping
Teton Range Wyoming early summer 1993

WILD = LIVING INDEPENDENTLY OF HUMANS

ROCK = SOLID PART OF EARTHS CRUST

(BOULDER Detached Rock
Glacial,

Boulder – Rounded mass of rock that has been shaped by erosion and transported by ice or water from original position. From old Swedish BULDER = rumbling

From "willed" came the adjective WILD used to convey the idea of being lost, unruly, disordered or confused.

ETYMOLOGICALLY "WILD-DÉOR-NESS" "The place of wild beasts." OLD ENGLISH

" I AM QUITE SERIOUSLY PROPOSING THAT WE GIVE LEGAL RIGHTS TO FORESTS, OCEANS, RIVERS AND OTHER SO-CALLED "NATURAL OBJECTS" IN THE ENVIRONMENT – INDEED THE NATURAL ENVIRONMENT AS A WHOLE."
CHRISTOPHER STONE 1972

"DO PEOPLE HAVE ETHICAL OBLIGATIONS TO ROCKS?"
LYNN WHITE 1973

Hamish Fulton. Notebook, 1993

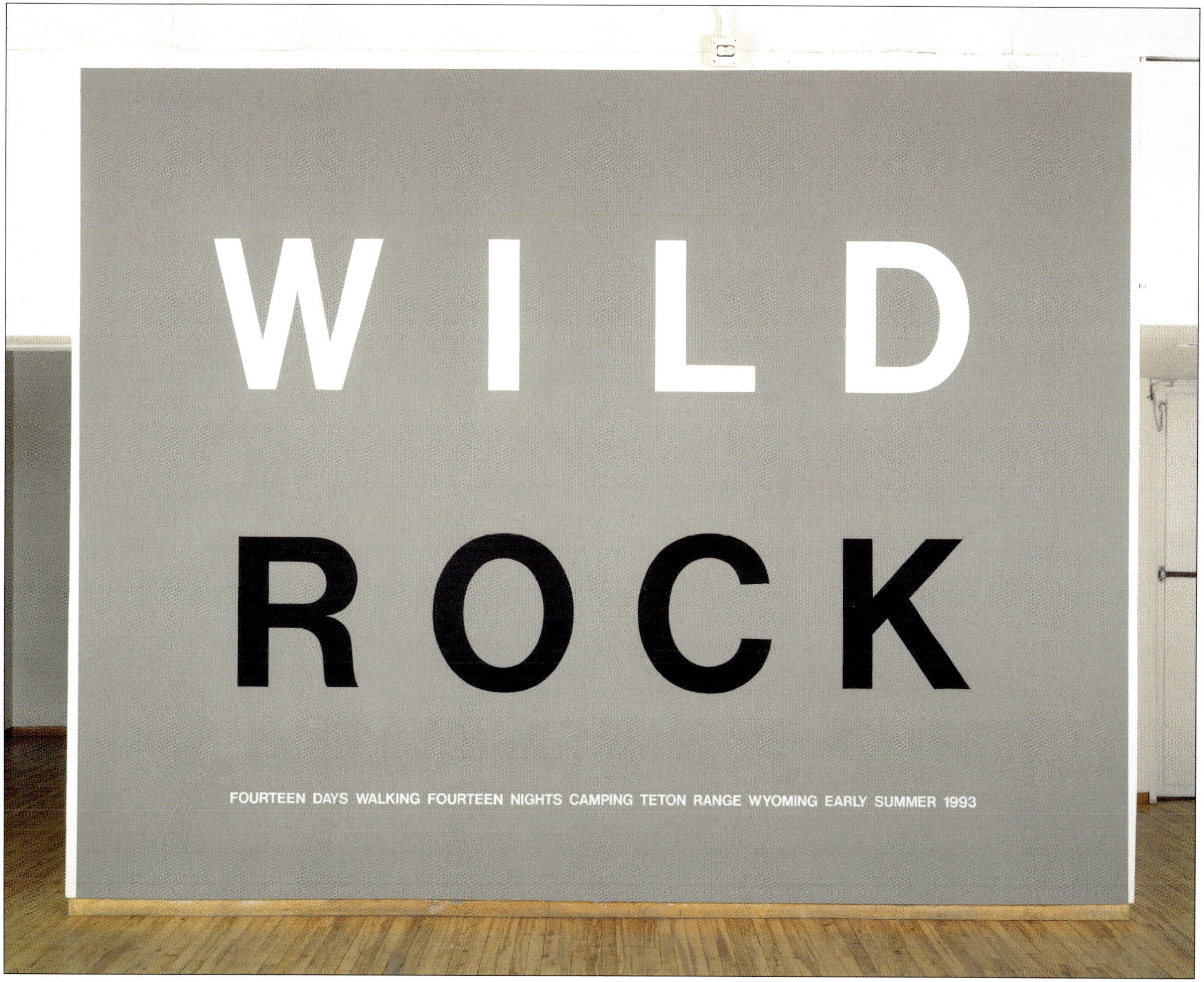

Hamish Fulton. WILD ROCK. Wall painting, 10'4" x 14'7". John Weber Gallery, New York, 1993

HAMISH FULTON—WALKING by Jay Griffiths

In Wales, traditionally, a traveller was never turned away without a meal and a rest, but the obligation fell upon her or him to bring news, stories or songs of other places. A gift for a gift. This is probably one of the most common of all human traditions, as I found when I walked the Highlands of West Papua. I was always given hospitality —and was always asked for news or for a song. Walkers in this way leave behind the realm of commerce and move into the world of gift.

For a foraging walk, such as Hamish Fulton's, relying on the gifts of nature, the land offers its hospitality, and a walker returns the favour with the gift of song, the journeyer's gift. Walking a landscape wakes the land and honours it, making its meaning and beauty more protected for being known. Fulton is also a guide, as the French word *passeur* explains, not just a mountain walker but a guide who can show the way, and his gift to the viewers of his work comes in the form of a whispered invitation: *walk the wild ways.*

The troubadours knew how to walk this way, those wandering singers who sang for their supper. The word 'troubadour' is a restless word, a turning word, a walking word, and its—disputed—etymology tells an entire and rich story. It probably combines meanings including the Arabic *tarrab* meaning 'to sing' and the Greek *tropos*, 'turn', and the Latin *turbare* 'to overturn'. Cognate with the French *trouver*, 'to find', the Occitan language offers the verb *trobar*, which means 'compose or invent'.

The history of walking is like the history of this one word 'troubadour': inventing, finding, singing up the turning world. And, indeed, with the quiet footpadding of a wolf, overturning the views of the sedentary establishment along the way.

Something of the troubadour wind whistles through the nomadism of ages: wayfarers, pilgrims, the Bohemian wanderers (those vagabond writer-philosophers and anti-establishment intellectuals), migrants, fugitives, travelling circuses, refugees and monks, the wandering Jews, Gypsies and nomadic cultures. The Romantics, particularly Wordsworth and Coleridge in the Lake District, chose to walk on the wildest side of their world, composing the songs and the attitude of opposition to the shibboleths of the establishment, and supporting the French Revolution's overturning of the *status quo*. When Fulton is described as a 'romantic anti-capitalist' he follows in these footsteps.

That word 'romantic' too is a wandering word, from the Medieval 'romance' that was a tale of chivalry, often in the form of a questing journey undertaken by a knight-errant; journeying in any wilderness the walker is knight-errant while the role of my lady, Greensleeves, is played by the wild and wide green world.

But the establishment has hated nomadism from the moment it first learned how to spit out the word. The Dominant Culture—wealthy, European-descent, men of estate, heterosexual, Christian and adult—have long marked one hated characteristic in their Other. The Other being, for them, the poor, non-European races, women, homosexuals, Gypsies, Jews, hunter-gatherers, the supposed insane and children. Along all the strata of power, there is a common factor: a hatred of nomadism.

A woman who is sexually free is termed a 'tramp', and a 'loose' woman is unfixed, liable to movement. According to a man in a sexist temper, women's conversation 'rambles.' We don't get to 'the point'. 'Wild women' in *Brewer's Dictionary of Phrase and Fable* from 1978 (first published in the nineteenth century) are those who 'go in for women's rights'—these wild women are 'runagates' who would 'stump the country'. (My grandmother was a Pankhurst—and I remain proud of all runagates.)

Vagrant, vagabond and tramp are all pejorative terms used on the very poor and all have nomadic overtones. A 'drifter' or 'transient' is a term of abuse. Adults speak disapprovingly of 'wayward' children and of teenagers being 'led astray'. Insane people are called 'unsettled,' 'disturbed' and 'unstable'—their mental mobility is considered a sickness. The people most persecuted by the Nazis shared the same—loathed—nomadic quality: Jews, a wandering people, an exiled people; the wandering Gypsies; and homosexuals who were wanderers across sexual bounds.

In Australia in 1888, the 'Aborigines' Protection Association' stated that any parent who 'roamed the country' should have their children stolen from them by the mission. The Aboriginal walkabout has been derided by white Australians, although it is a profound physical and psychological practice, and one necessary to survival. In 1910 in Canada, the French missionary Father Le Clercq commented that the 'wandering and vagabond life' must be brought to an end, so that he could 'render the savages sedentary.' Seeking to colonise the Native Americans, the settlers imprisoned the survivors in reservations.

All of this history lies behind Fulton's 1969 walk over the Little Big Horn battlefield, where the Sioux defeated the US government troops in 1876. He was following in the footsteps of Sitting Bull and, more widely, in the footsteps of all wild walkers who have known the political resistance inherent in roaming.

But most, if not all, culture-heroes travel: the Aboriginal Ancestors, Odysseus, Beowulf, Don Quixote. Arguably, leaving one's community to travel is a necessity for full development, for the lure of wild and nomadic freedom has never left us, any of us. It is in our lungs, breathing in freedom, in our eyes, hungry for horizons and in our feet, itching for the open road. Put your seven-league boots on. To 'wander' is the Taoist code word for becoming ecstatic, and roamers, farfarers and wayfarers know the intoxication.

Shadow the wild cat as it walks by his wild lone in the freedom of the wilds.

In walking is freedom: the freedom to pass or pause; the freedom to stop an hour by the gorse that smells of coconut; the freedom to find your own speed and your own way. Walking frees the body from its seated, sedentary muscle-jams, and walking is both common and free, although in practice for many today it is both rare and priceless. People speak of longing to go walking when time 'permits' or when work 'allows' it. To do something for free is itself, in these days of turbo-capitalism, a kind of gentle revolution.

The body's freedom encourages the freedom of the spirit, too, the open-hearted, wide-minded freedom we are born to, the *Liberté* indeed that was a rallying cry of the French Revolution. One of the creations of the French Republic was a new calendar that honoured not the establishment church and the established dynasties of empire but rather a pagan, countryside calendar, the turning world of nature's months, the nomadic year walking through its seasons of snow, rain, wind, turning in spring through the seasons of sprouting and flowering, by summer becoming meadow and harvest, then the days of heat, fruit and vintage until the seasons of mist and frost return the snows again.

The days were named too, to honour plants, minerals, animals and simple tools. Fulton's day of departure in the Cairngorms, April 18th, is the day of the blueberry, for instance, followed by days dedicated to 'knife', 'rose', 'oak', 'fern' and 'hawthorn'. It is as if the calendar asks one to aspire to the Buddhistic 'Be Here and Now' in this actual world of nature and nature's time, not the artifice of empires and abstract gods, and each republican day honours such republican deities as slate or ash or wheelbarrow. The hawthorn will, in one form or another, influence the whole of Fulton's walk, for the name of the River Spey, running through the Cairngorms, is derived from the Celtic meaning 'hawthorn stream'.

Walking always encourages the walker to be fully present and in time with the rhythms of the earth. For Earth itself is a walker and at the latitude of the Cairngorms she will be walking at about, say, seven hundred miles per hour, turning, turning her troubadour ways. Walking, the high tide of sunrise wakes you and evening's low tide lets you slip into the sea of sleep. Walking draws you towards the pace of the voyaging day, and walking sets your tempo with the speeds of the places and creatures one might meet—the *adagio* lochs, the vivacious *allegría* of an otter, an eagle in a *ritardando* circling in the air currents. *Andante*, *andante*, the man, of course, *andante* the human walking speed, *andante* the breathing as regular as heart pace and foot pace. Breathing is our first reciprocity with the world—the first and primal gift. Your breath goes out into the world and the world's breath returns into you.

In walking, a great metamorphosis can happen—walking can prevent the sclerosis of emotional cages, walking can break you free of the confines of hurt and anger. There is reported to be a custom among the Inuit whereby a person, seized with anger, may walk out their rage, striding out in a straight line until their anger dissolves, at which point a stick may be left to mark the distance, a testimony to the intensity of their fury. Eco-psychology too tells us that walking in nature is a treatment for depression, and walking, as pilgrimage, is part of many spiritual disciplines. Every walk teaches that in the turning world, 'this too will pass.'

Some of the world's most extraordinary journeyers are the 'Marathon Monks' of Mount Hiei in Japan: Buddhist monks who, during the course of seven years, will run nearly thirty thousand miles, a distance greater than the circumference of the Earth. When they have run the entire and turning world, they attain enlightenment (and deserve it). But before they put on their seven-league boots, though, they must master seated meditation, focusing on the deep breathing that is at the heart of their physical and spiritual discipline. Chanting and rhythmic skills are involved, the beat of the mantra, the breath and the footsteps all synchronised.

There is a similar Tibetan tradition, the 'Lung-gom-pa,' or 'Wind Meditation', a practice of running by which the lamas seemed to fly, to run by trance-light. They could cover perhaps two hundred miles in a day, and could keep running for two days solid. There was a strong emphasis on breath-control and visualization, as the lamas would imagine themselves being as light as a feather in the winds. Another and telling aspect of their training was to learn to keep their eyes fixed on a single star.

They were often messengers, too, a word of both social and spiritual freight, for, as journeyers, relying on alms or gifts, they brought their own gifts in turn, of news or messages. The word for messenger, in Greek, is *angellos*, from which we get the word 'angel'.

In another sense, though, the act of wild walking carries a message. The messenger is the message, and the message he or she delivers is the message of slow, deep metamorphosis by which landscape is inwritten into the human being. For the marathon monks, the final attainment is that 'At the end, the marathon monk has become one with the mountain.' Something of this is knowable to all walkers: the walker enters the world and the world the walker.

You are where you have walked. Walking, the wind becomes your breath. Walking inscribes itself into the whole body of the walker. Paths, once walked, create the sinews. Streams, drunk, enter the veins. Rocks, climbed, form the calluses of hands. Twisted tree roots curl up the body in muscle. Packed earth, tramped, becomes compacted vigour. The eyes? What of the eyes? They hold the skies, all the skies they have ever seen. The walker, turning in the troubadour way, singing and finding and gleaning, finds the land is growing, murmuring and turning within.

This is the ultimate reciprocal breath, in and out, as light as air, as free as wind, as clear as water, a gift-exchange as easy as light through glass, where what is finally achieved is transparency. Reckless, lovely transparency, where everything passes and the passeur and the pass are translucent to each other, a transparency as perfect and as simple as water and air and wind.

Jay Griffiths is the author of Wild: An Elemental Journey

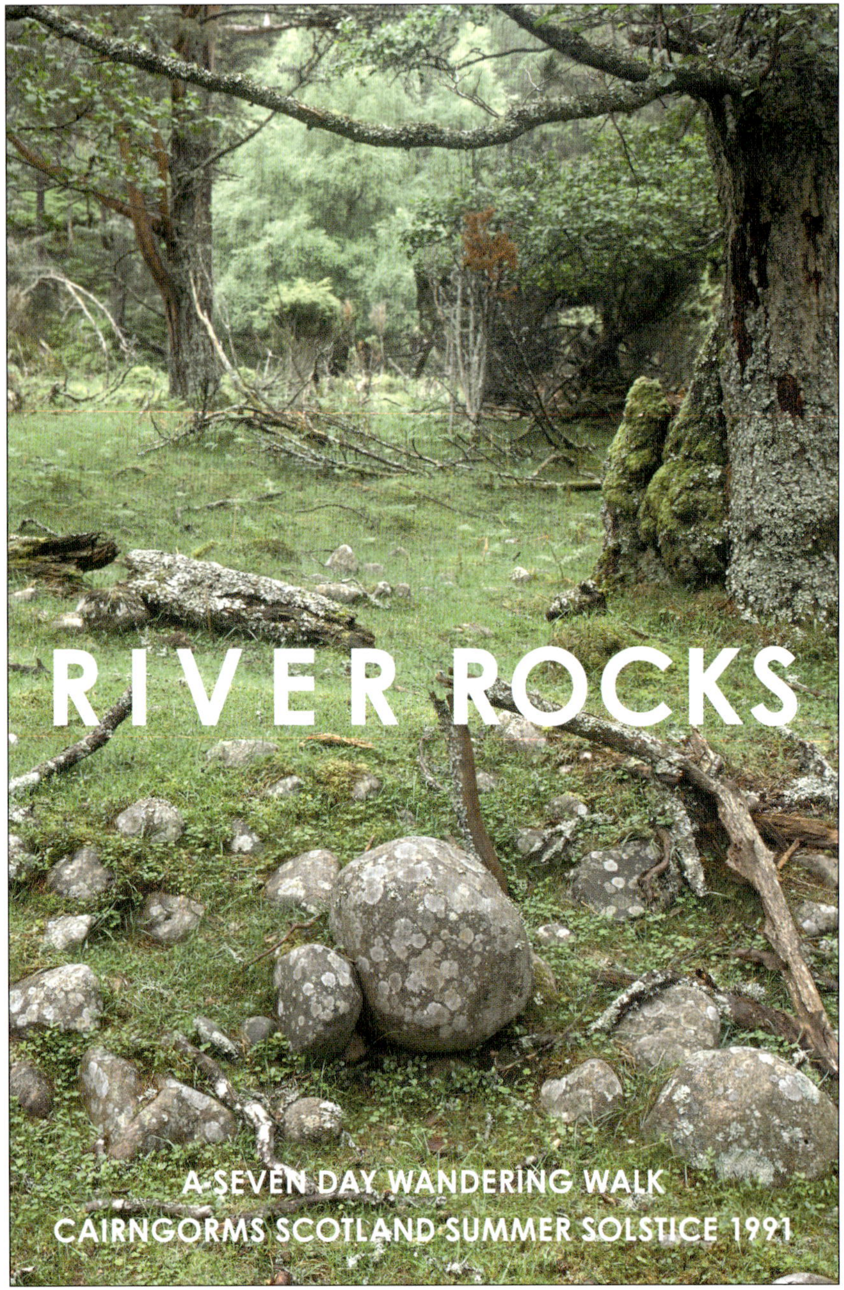
RIVER ROCKS
A SEVEN DAY WANDERING WALK
CAIRNGORMS SCOTLAND SUMMER SOLSTICE 1991

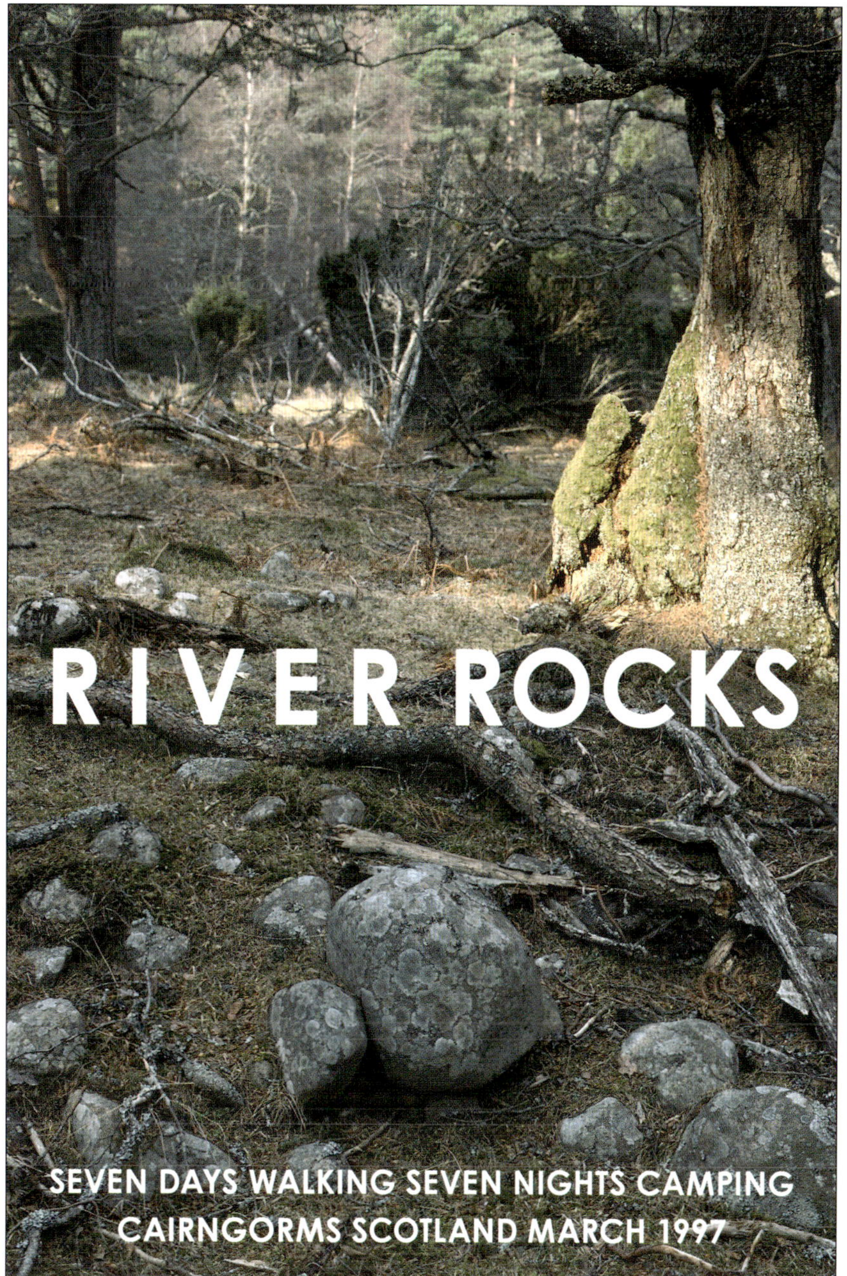
RIVER ROCKS
SEVEN DAYS WALKING SEVEN NIGHTS CAMPING
CAIRNGORMS SCOTLAND MARCH 1997

A SEVEN DAY WANDERING WALK CAIRNGORMS SCOTLAND MARCH 1991

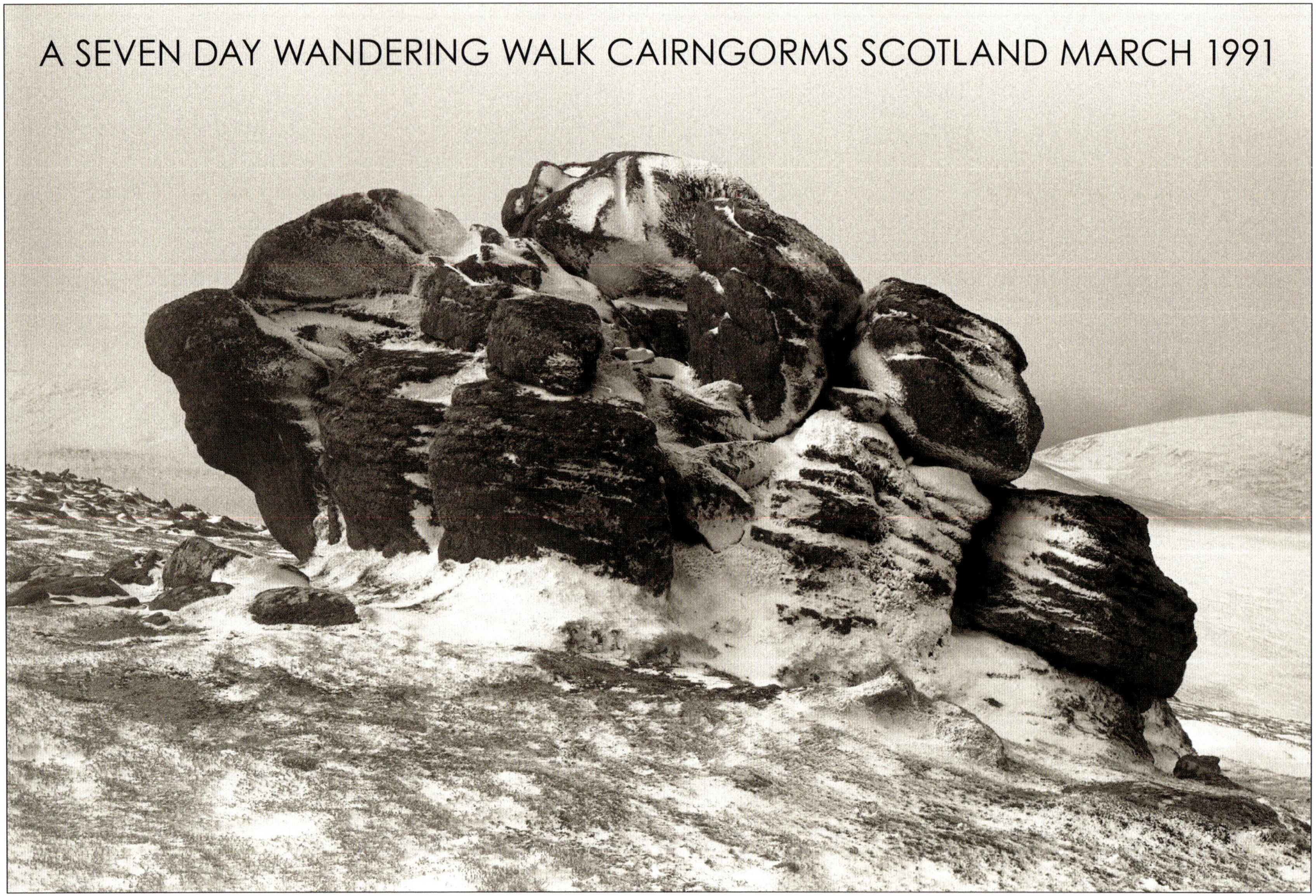

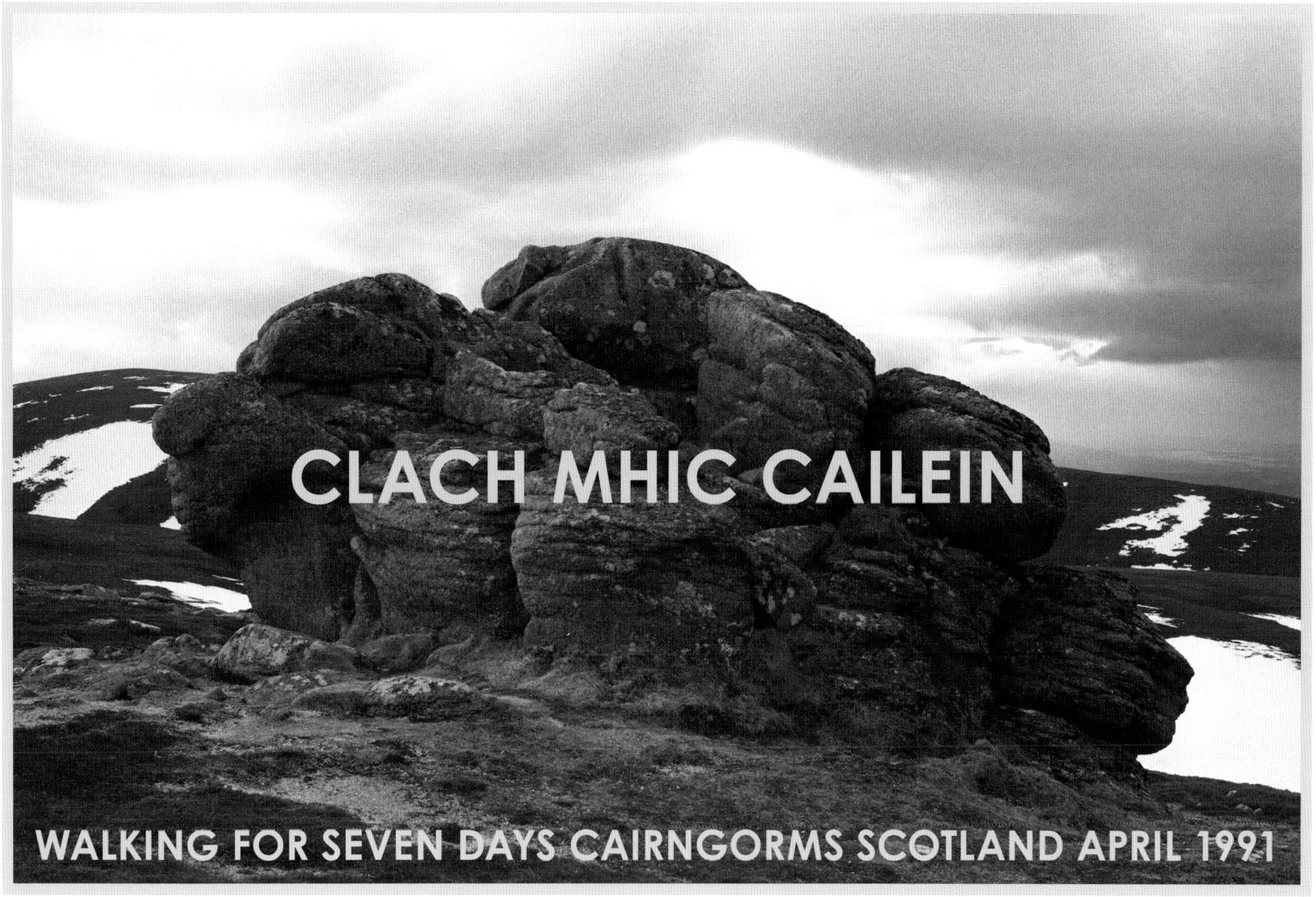
CLACH MHIC CAILEIN
WALKING FOR SEVEN DAYS CAIRNGORMS SCOTLAND APRIL 1991

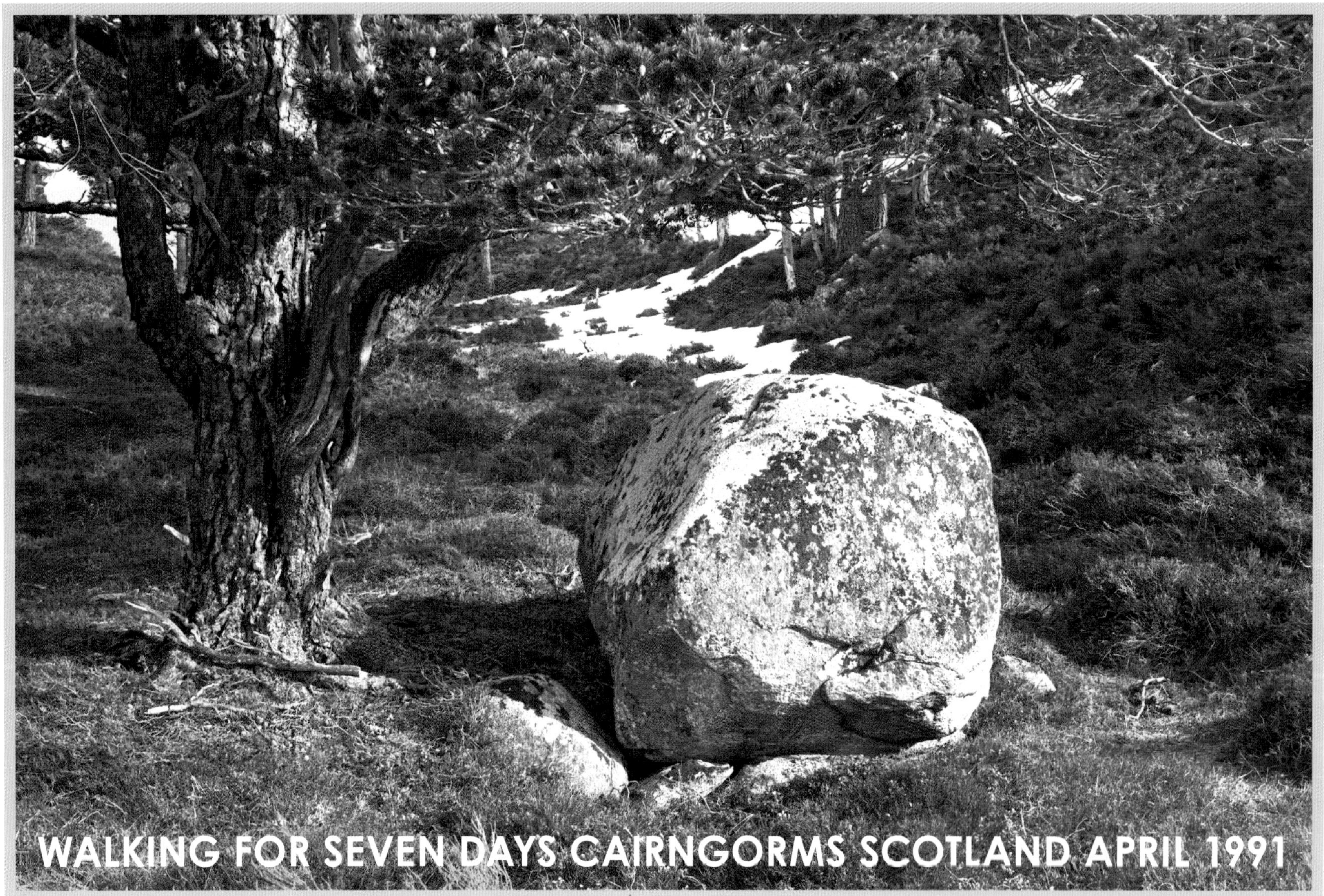
WALKING FOR SEVEN DAYS CAIRNGORMS SCOTLAND APRIL 1991

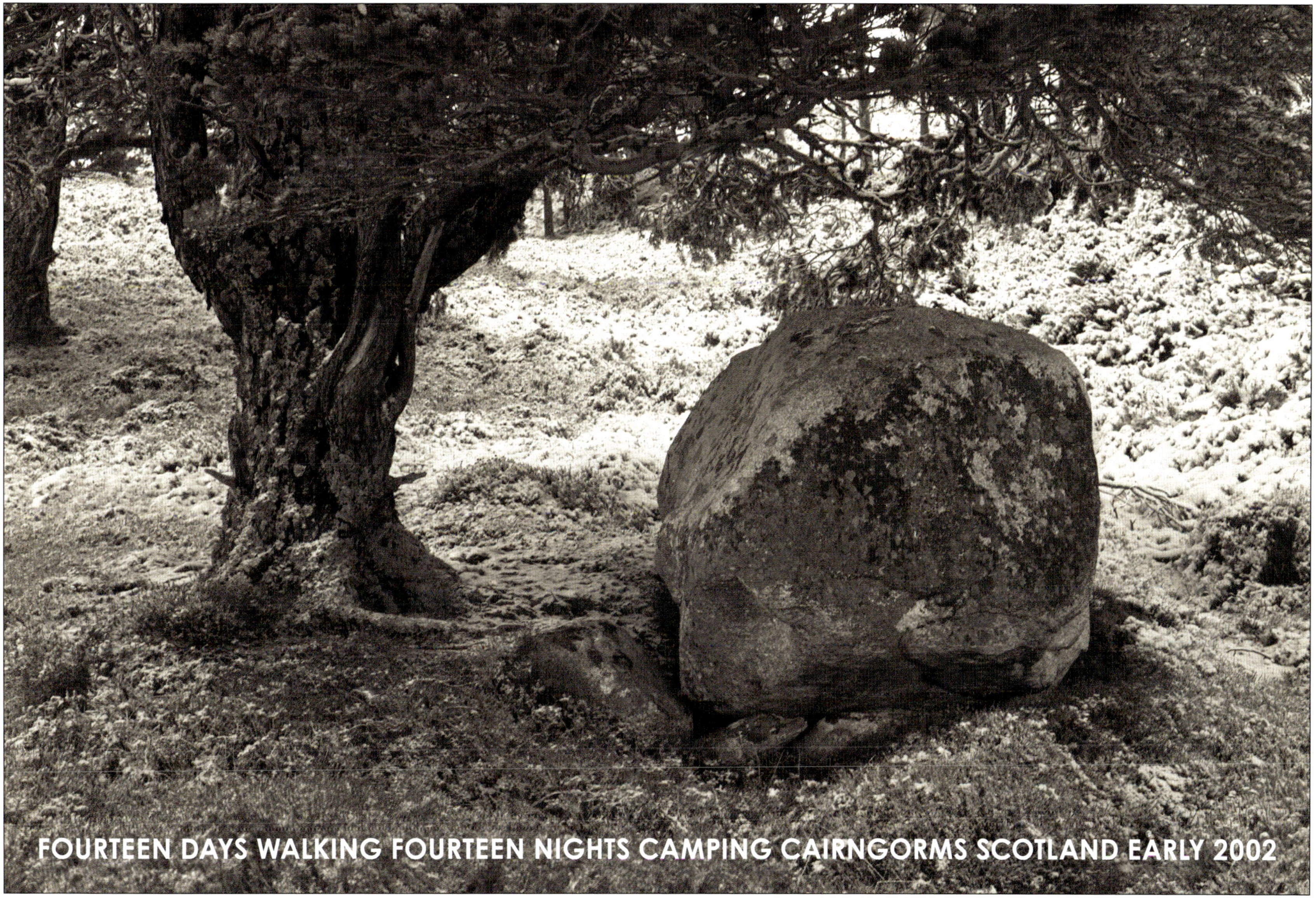
FOURTEEN DAYS WALKING FOURTEEN NIGHTS CAMPING CAIRNGORMS SCOTLAND EARLY 2002

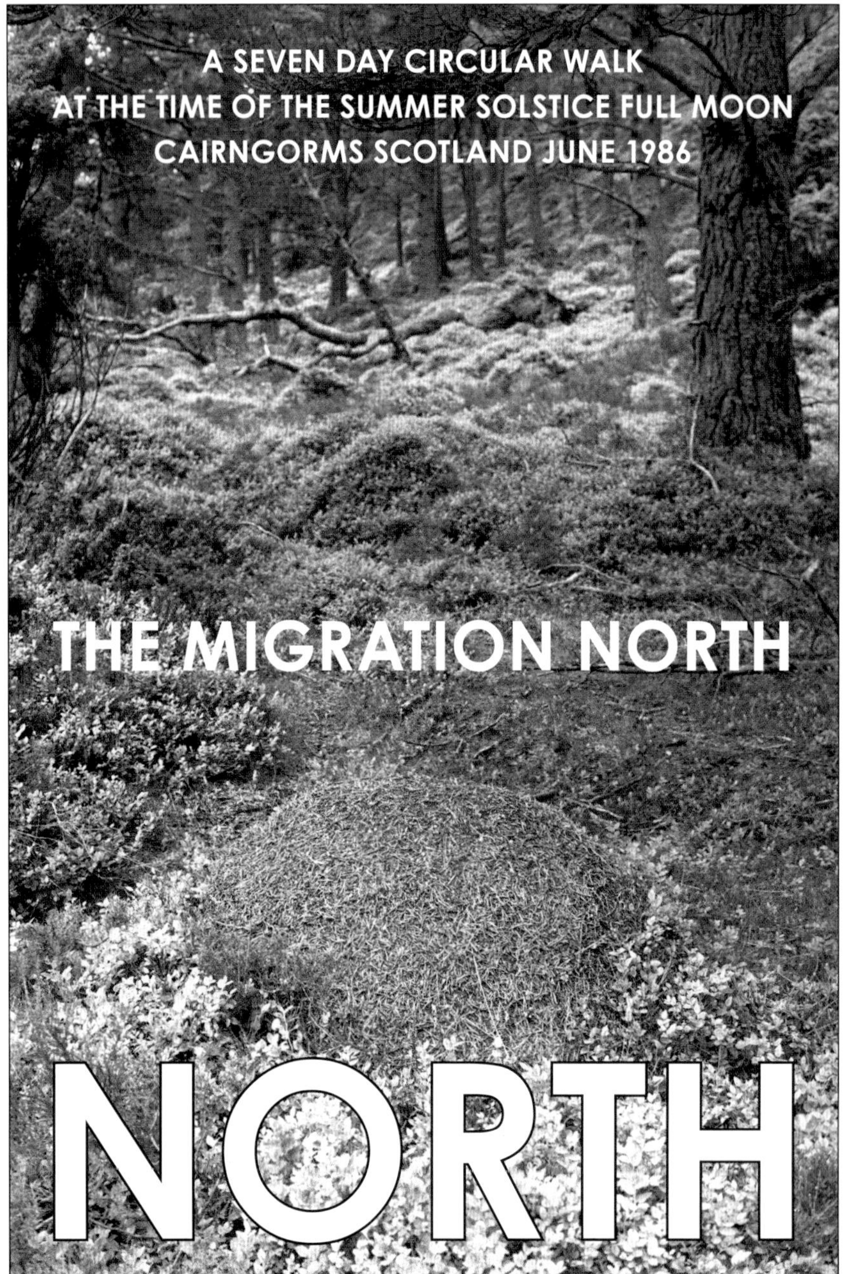
A SEVEN DAY CIRCULAR WALK
AT THE TIME OF THE SUMMER SOLSTICE FULL MOON
CAIRNGORMS SCOTLAND JUNE 1986
THE MIGRATION NORTH
NORTH

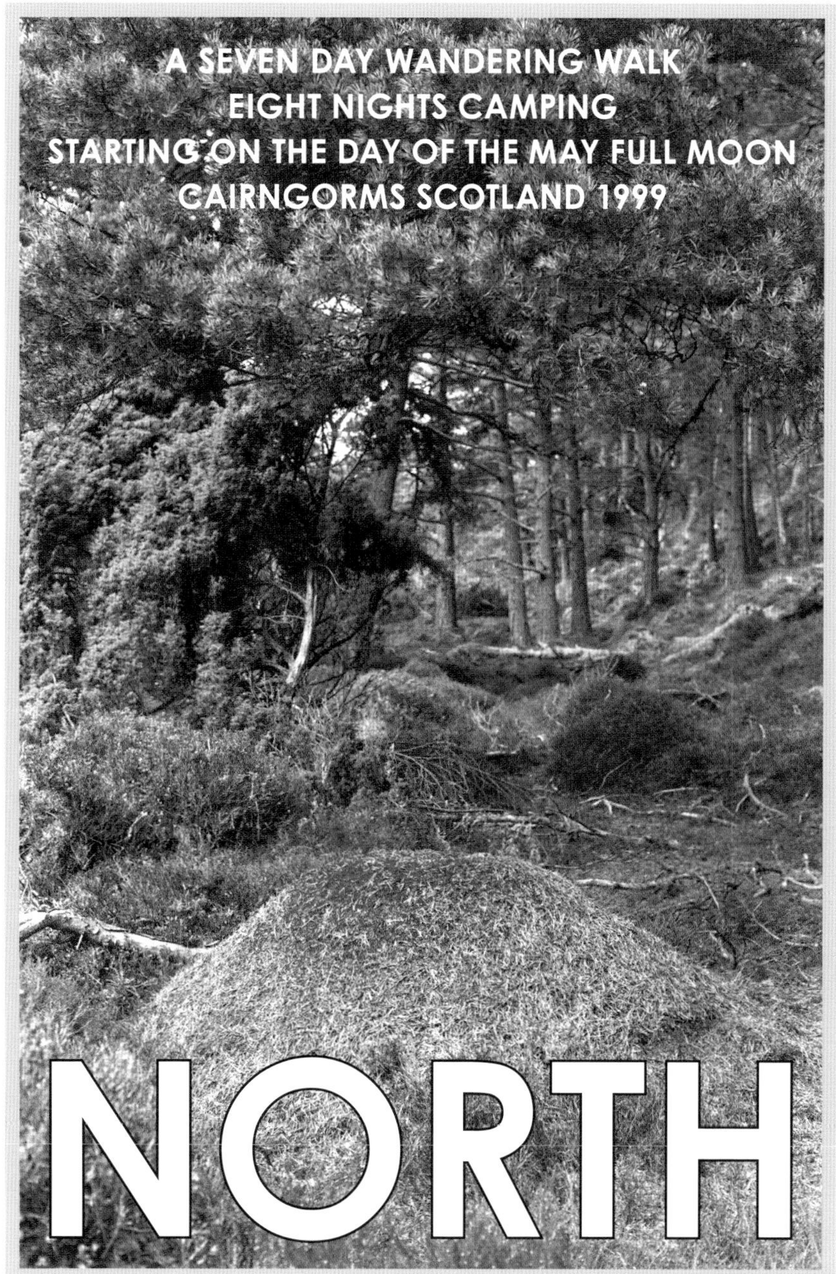
A SEVEN DAY WANDERING WALK
EIGHT NIGHTS CAMPING
STARTING ON THE DAY OF THE MAY FULL MOON
CAIRNGORMS SCOTLAND 1999
NORTH

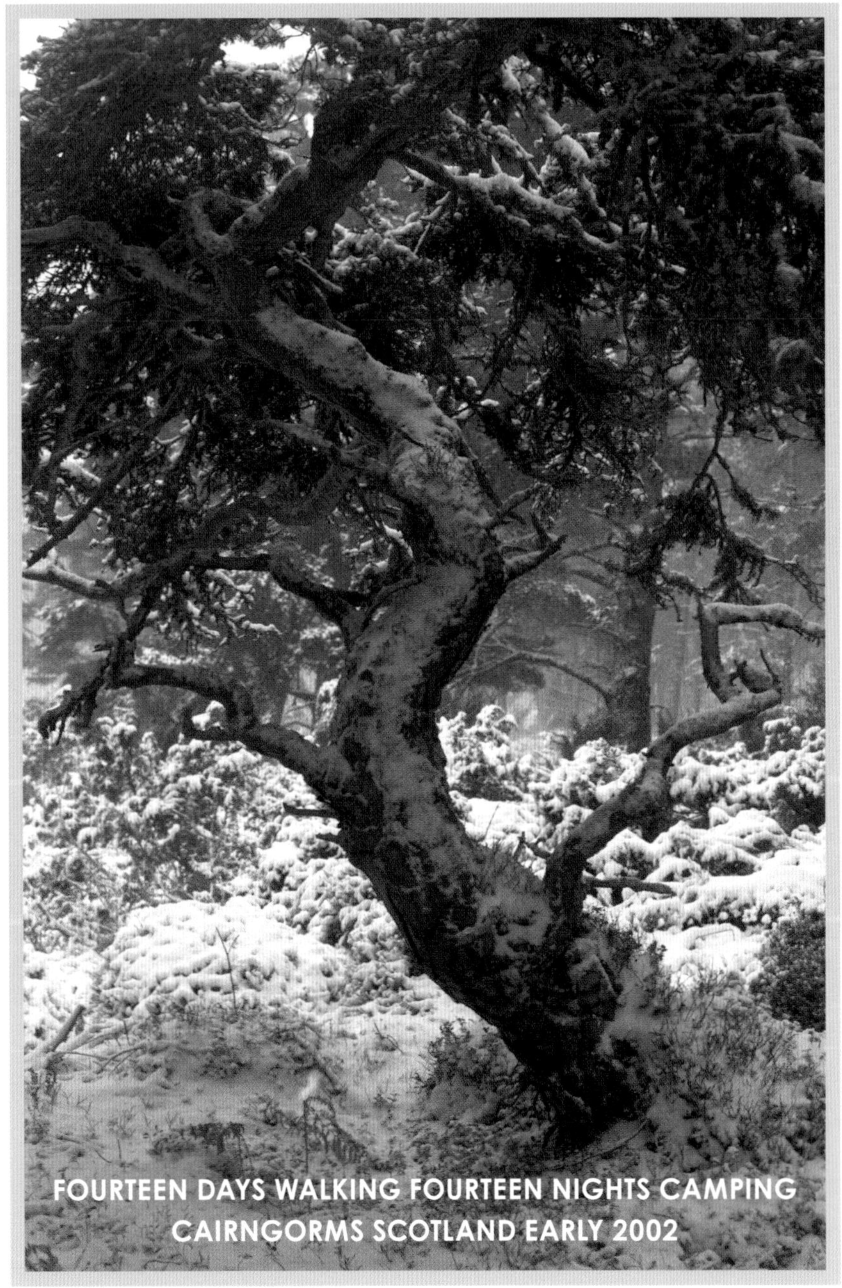
FOURTEEN DAYS WALKING FOURTEEN NIGHTS CAMPING
CAIRNGORMS SCOTLAND EARLY 2002

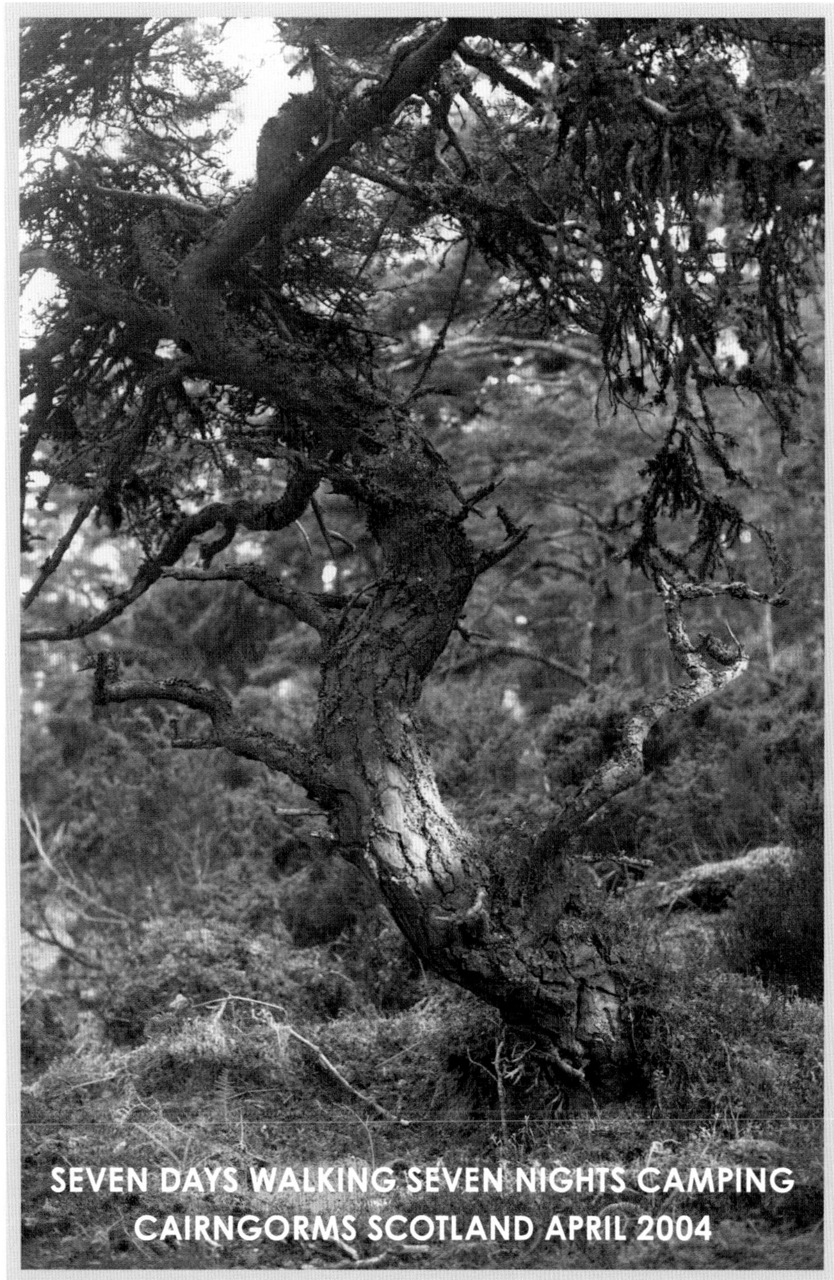
SEVEN DAYS WALKING SEVEN NIGHTS CAMPING
CAIRNGORMS SCOTLAND APRIL 2004

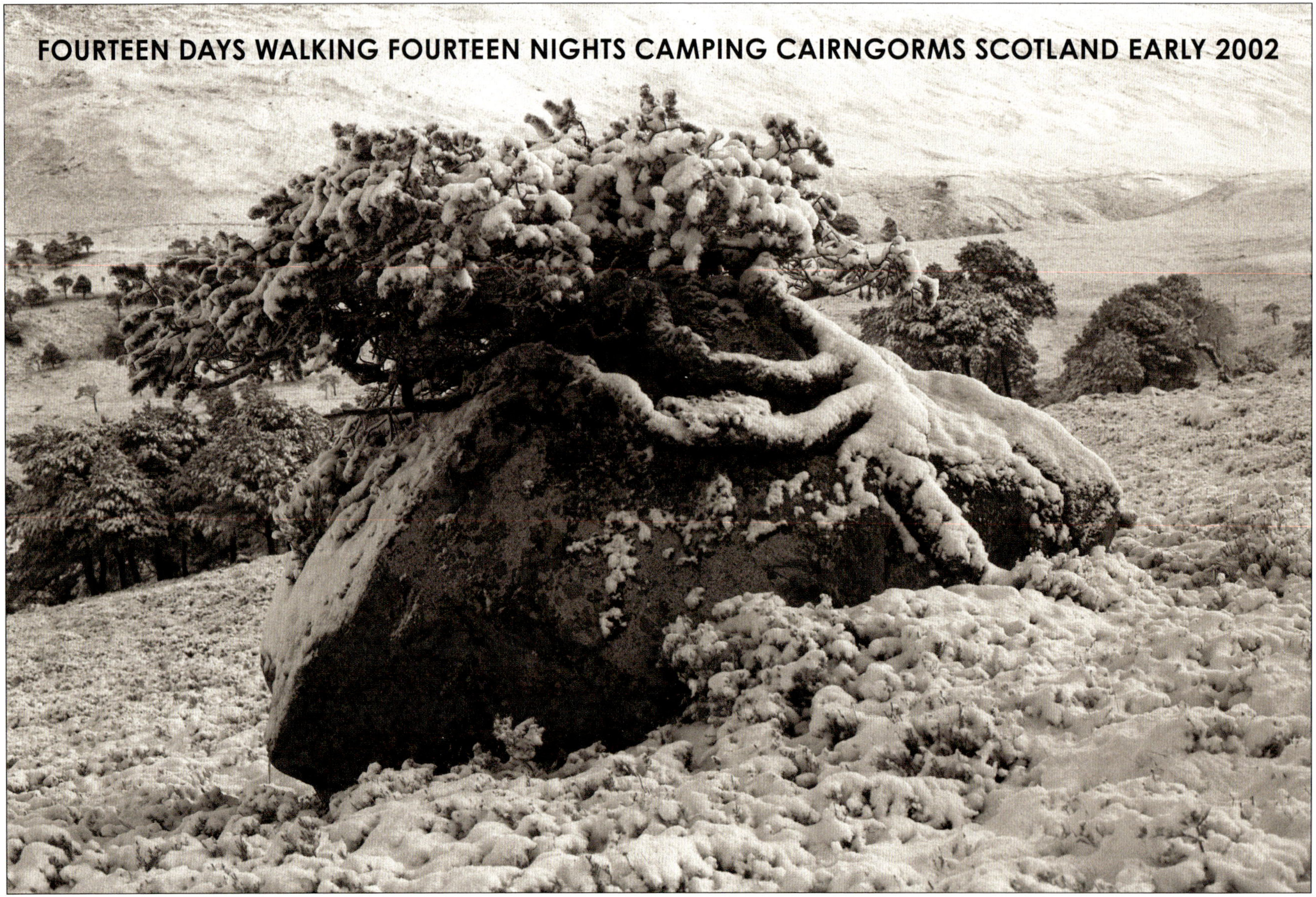
FOURTEEN DAYS WALKING FOURTEEN NIGHTS CAMPING CAIRNGORMS SCOTLAND EARLY 2002

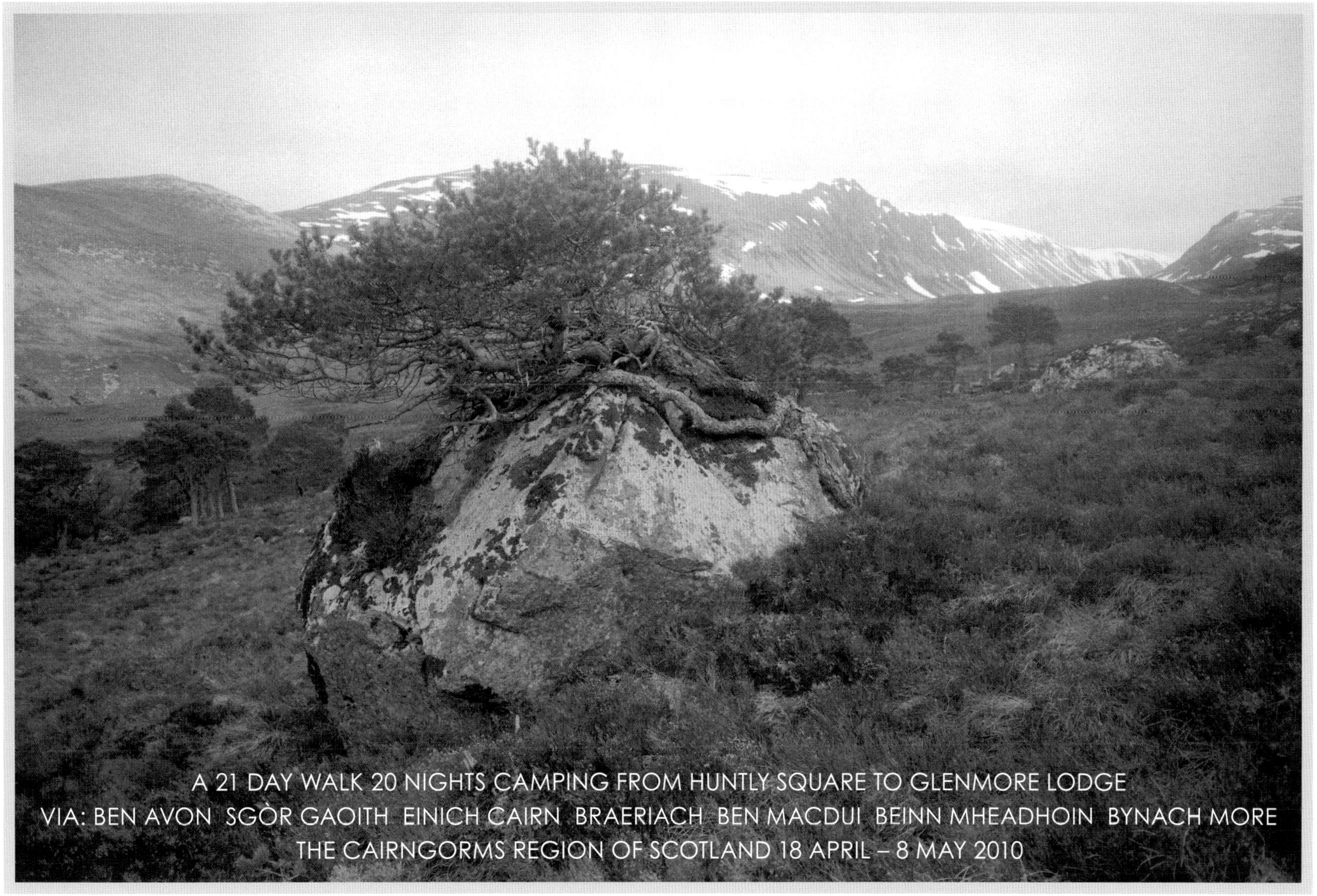
A 21 DAY WALK 20 NIGHTS CAMPING FROM HUNTLY SQUARE TO GLENMORE LODGE
VIA: BEN AVON SGÒR GAOITH EINICH CAIRN BRAERIACH BEN MACDUI BEINN MHEADHOIN BYNACH MORE
THE CAIRNGORMS REGION OF SCOTLAND 18 APRIL – 8 MAY 2010

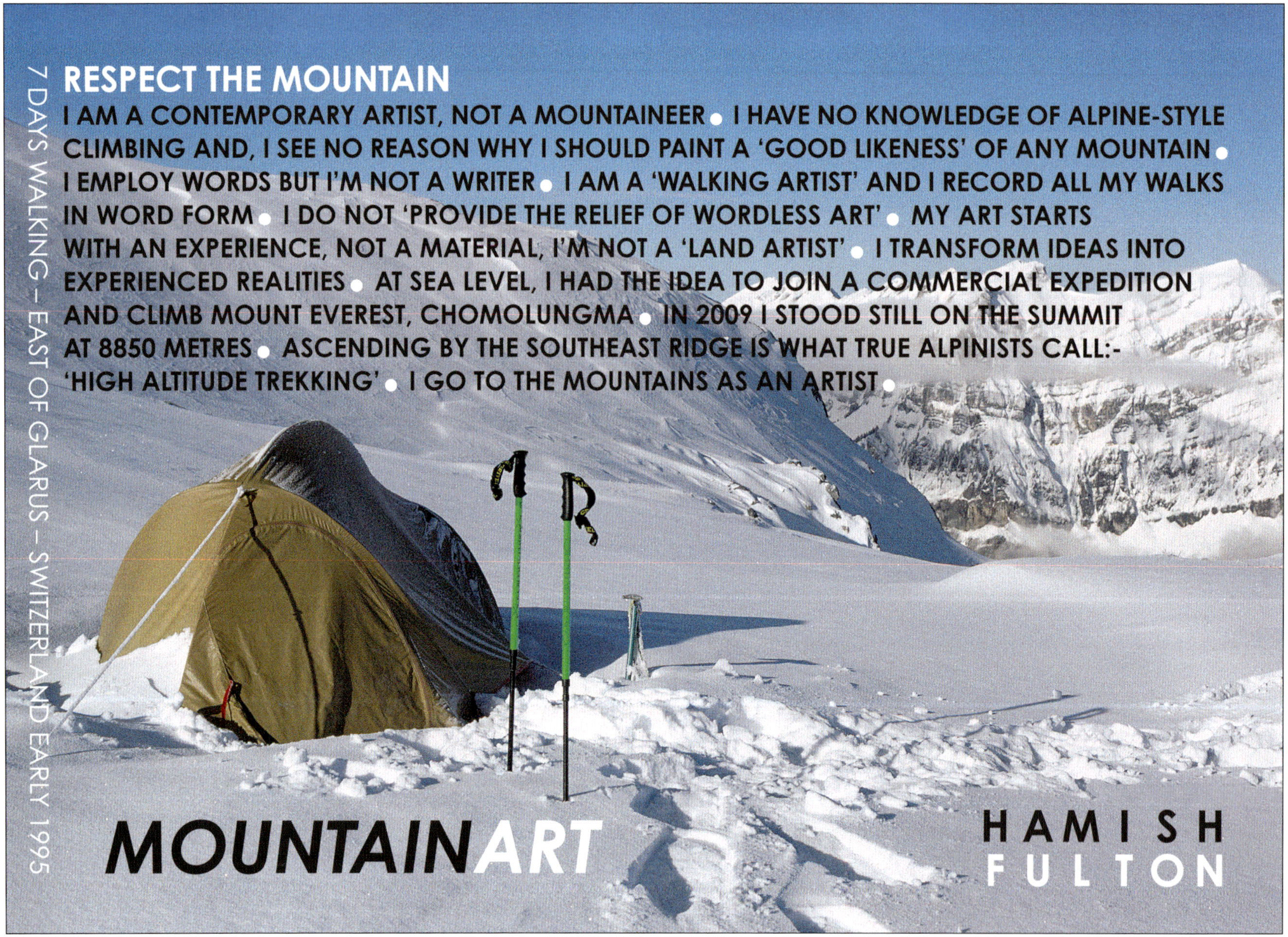

Hamish Fulton announcement card. *Rispetta La Montagna*. Museo Transfrontaliero del Monte Bianco, Courmayeur Valle d'Aosta, 2010

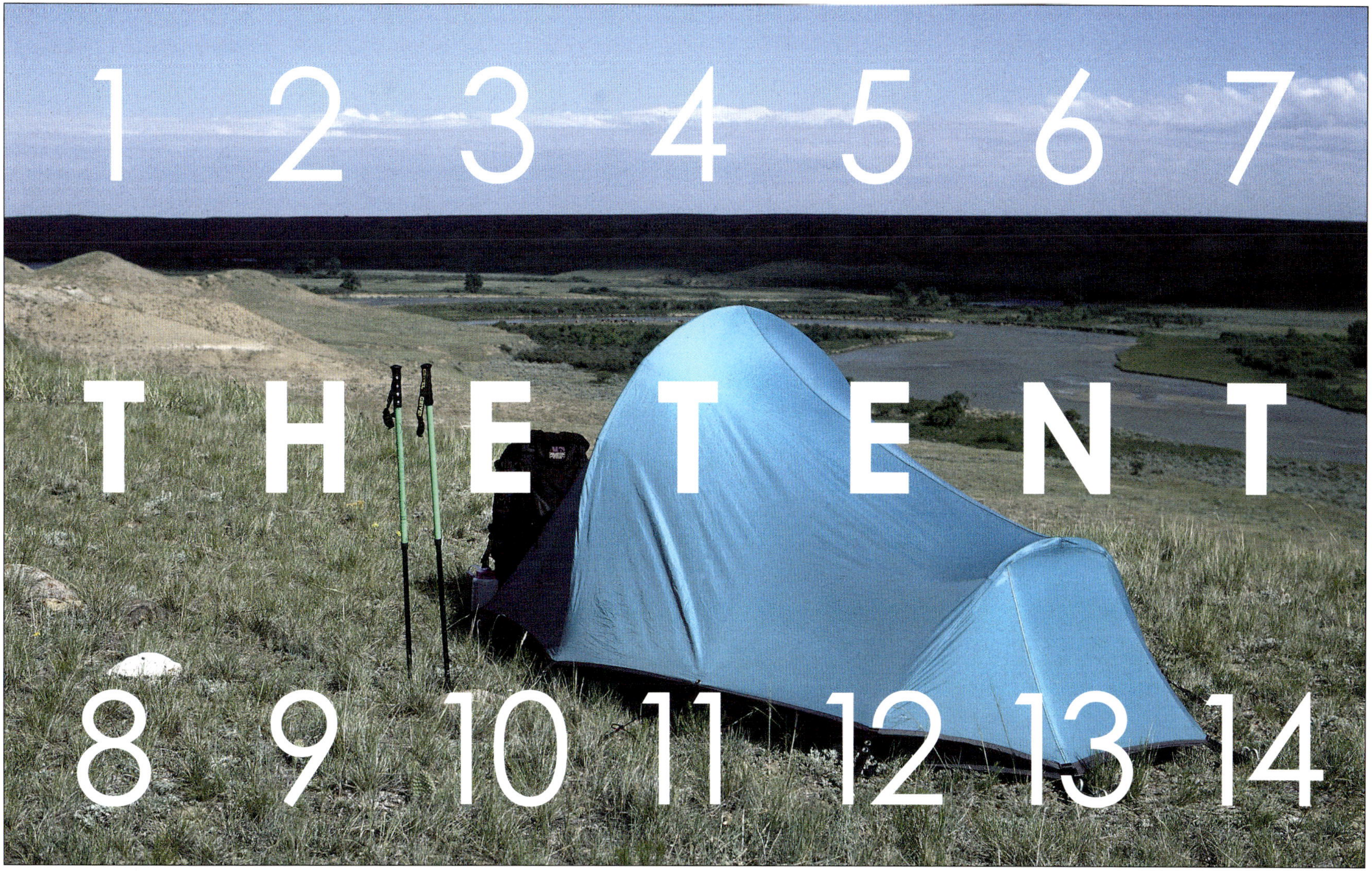

COUNTING 28 BAREFOOT PACES WALKING ROUND A TIPI RING

A 14 DAY WALKING JOURNEY 14 NIGHTS CAMPING ALONG THE NORTH SHORES AND OVER BLUFFS OF THE MILK RIVER

DOWNSTREAM RETURNING UPSTREAM STARTING ON THE SEVENTH DAY OF THE SEVENTH MONTH

TENT DOORS FACING THE SUNRISE EACH DAY ALBERTA CANADA 1999

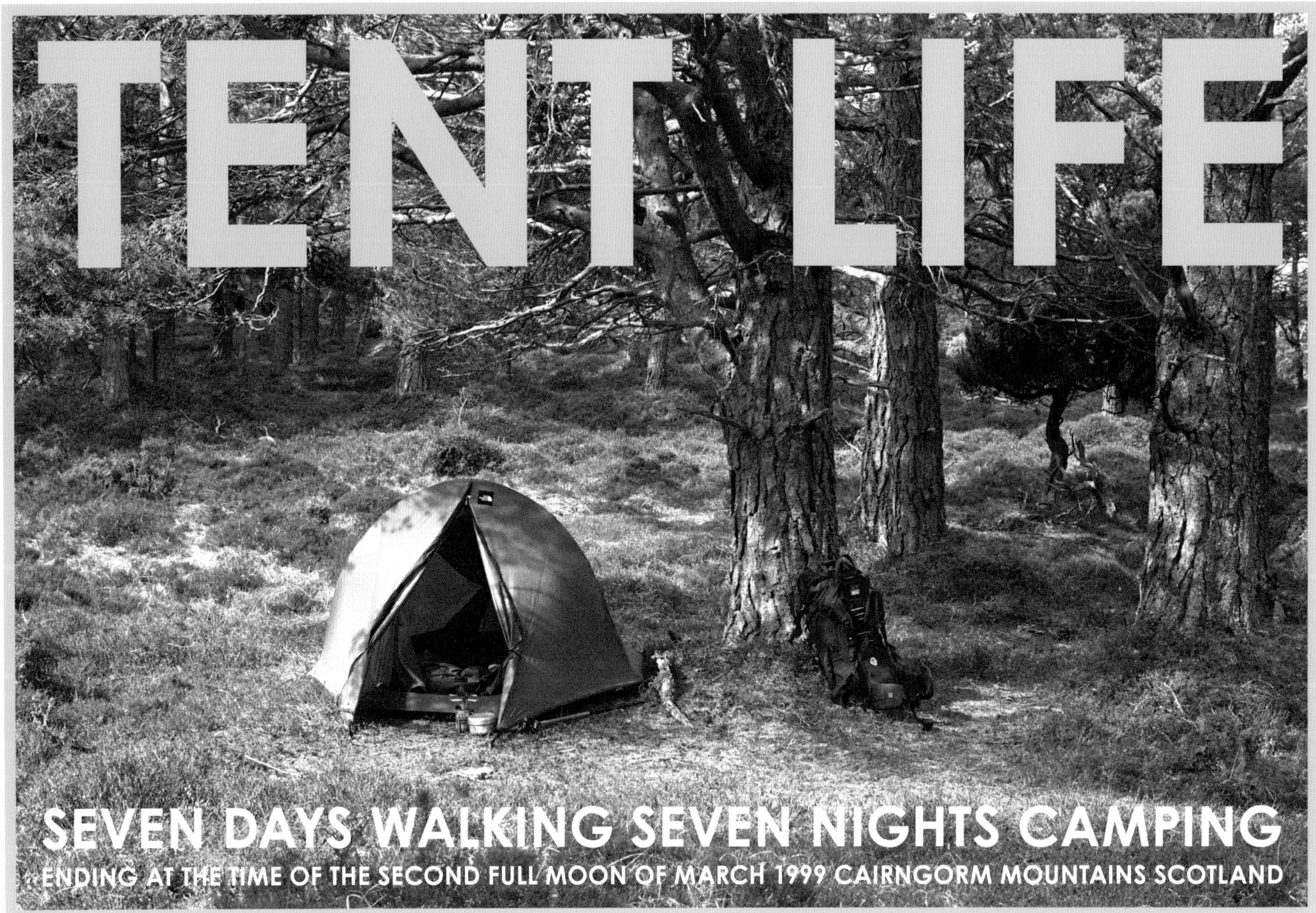
TENT LIFE
SEVEN DAYS WALKING SEVEN NIGHTS CAMPING
ENDING AT THE TIME OF THE SECOND FULL MOON OF MARCH 1999 CAIRNGORM MOUNTAINS SCOTLAND

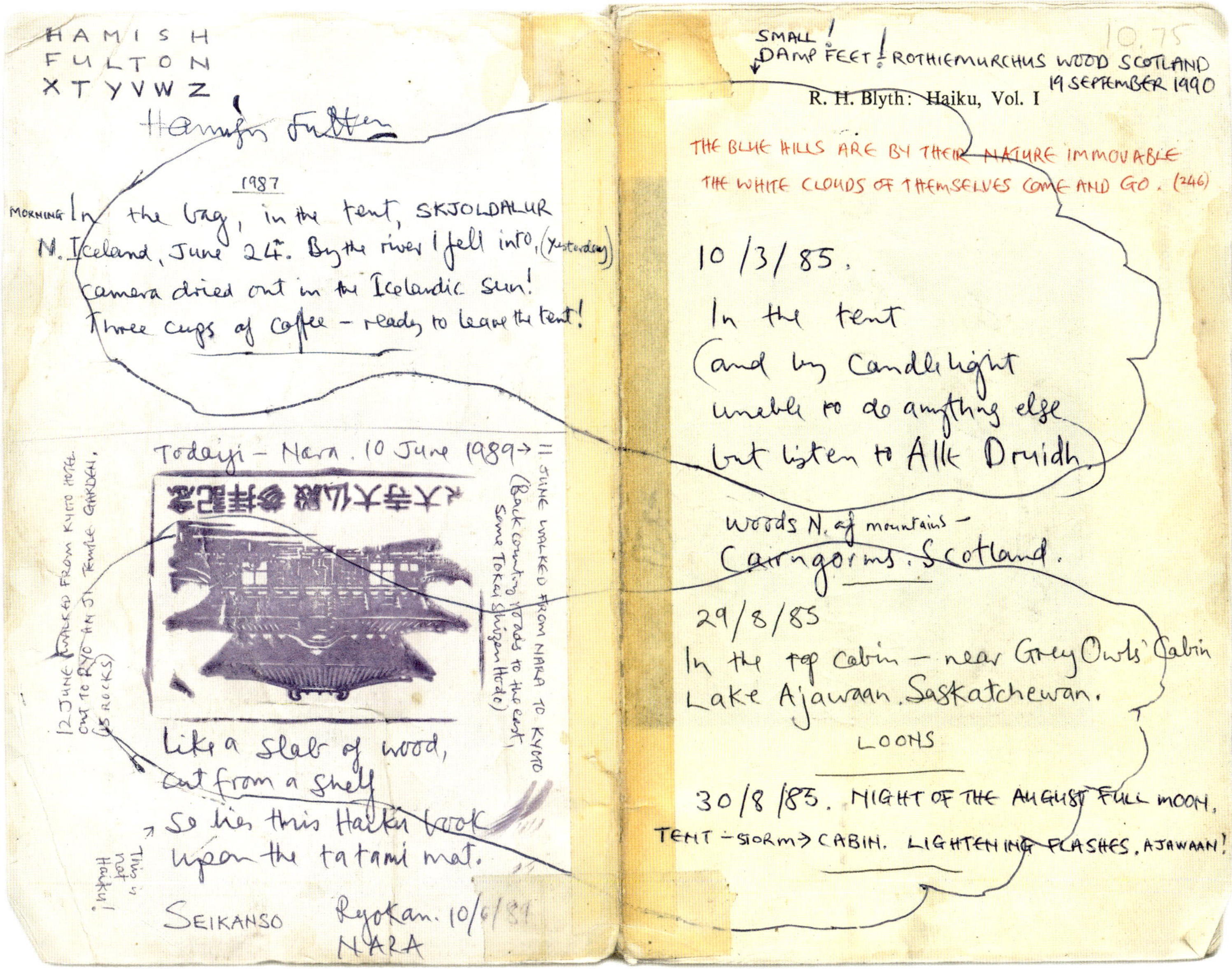

R. H. Blyth: Haiku Volume I. 1949 (Paperback edition 1981)

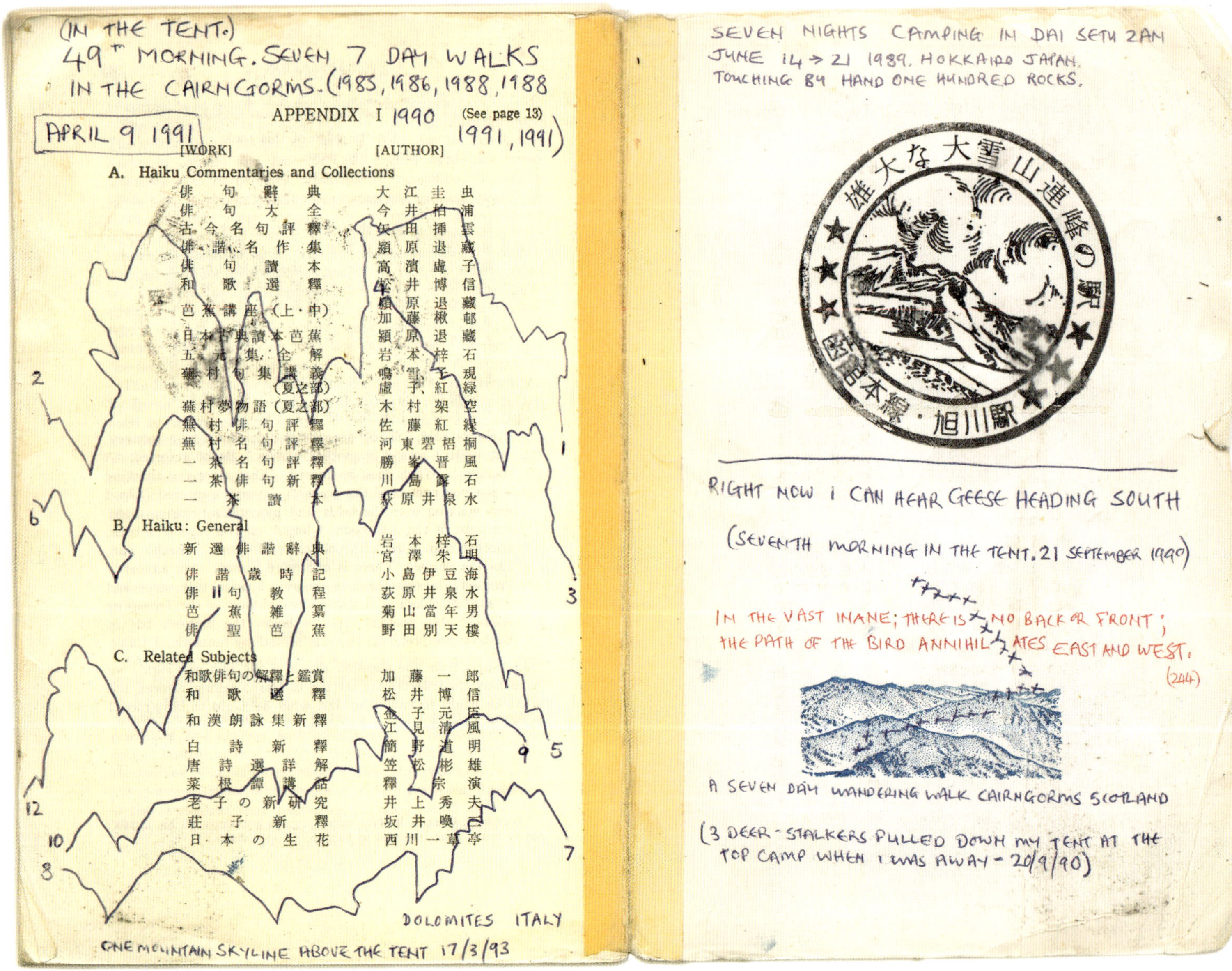

R. H. Blyth: Haiku Volume I. 1949 (Paperback edition 1981)

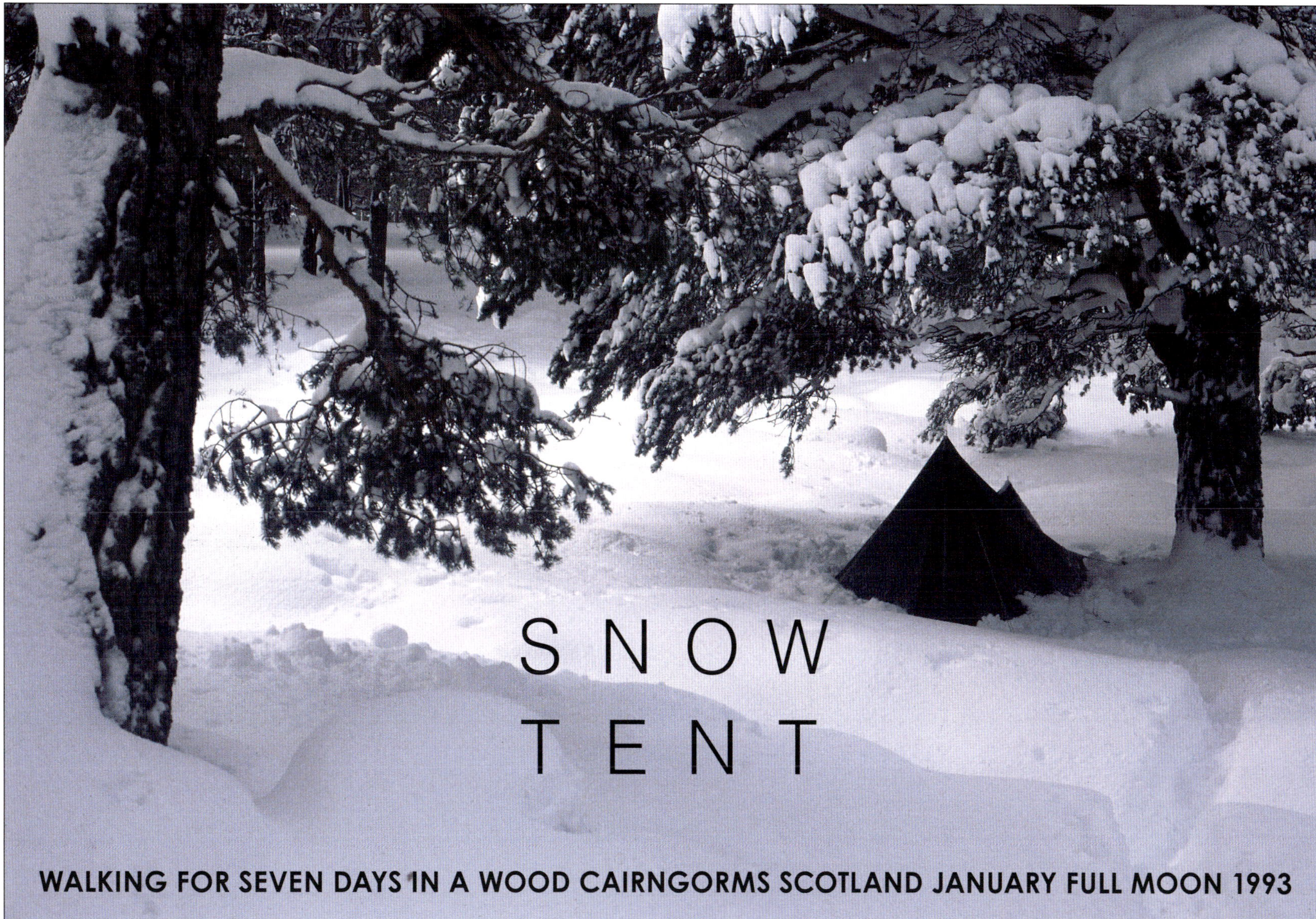
SNOW
TENT
WALKING FOR SEVEN DAYS IN A WOOD CAIRNGORMS SCOTLAND JANUARY FULL MOON 1993

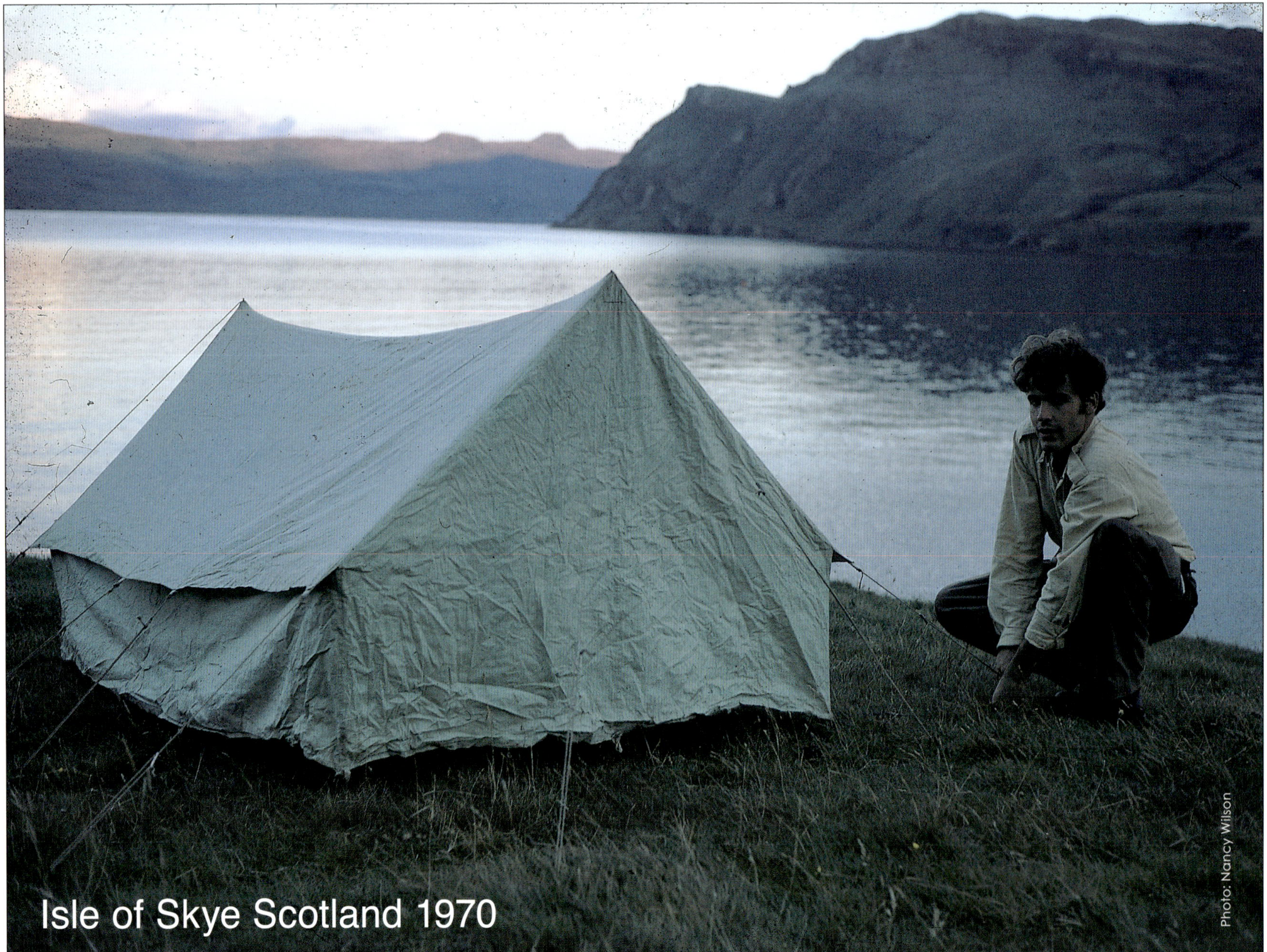
Isle of Skye Scotland 1970
Photo: Nancy Wilson

CONFORM IS A SEVEN-LETTER WORD

29 June 2010 just before leaving England to install my small exhibition of mountain art at Courmayeur in Northern Italy (see page 30), I picked up a copy of *Beyond The Mountain* by the American alpinist Steve House (born 1970). In the chapter titled "A Punk in Crampons", he says, "My college classmates write from their graduate school jobs with tales of endless titrations completed in science labs, of 80-hour weeks researching their professor's theses. I slowly kick steps up 20,000-foot volcanoes and resent my lack of intellectual challenge. Knowing my goals are solely mine, I scoff at those who went to grad school, or took so-called real jobs. That is the ultimate sell out: to work for the man. To cast your own soul into a hell of cubicles and workstations and dollar bills. And if they don't see this, they don't deserve the chance to find out who they might become." I am a contemporary artist, not a mountaineer and certainly not an alpinist – but somehow that paragraph struck a chord.

In May 2009, I was as they say, "led like a dog on a leash" (not 'by fair means') up to the 8850-metre summit of Mount Everest with a commercial expedition. This unbelievably lucky fact does not make me a mountaineer but I did *TRAVERSE* from the 'art world' comfort zone across to → my mountain mind, before – during – after.

In 1970, when I was twenty-four years old, I quit my teaching job. At that moment, I wanted out of employment, to rid myself of guilt. "First you must know what you want to do!" I wanted to commit myself to the life of an artist, a walking artist. (A direction that was finally clarified in 1973 after a one-thousand-mile walk.) Occasionally someone will say to me – "It's all very well for you, making all these walks, but I have to work. I just don't have the time (to make a 21-day walk)." I made my decisions and they made theirs.

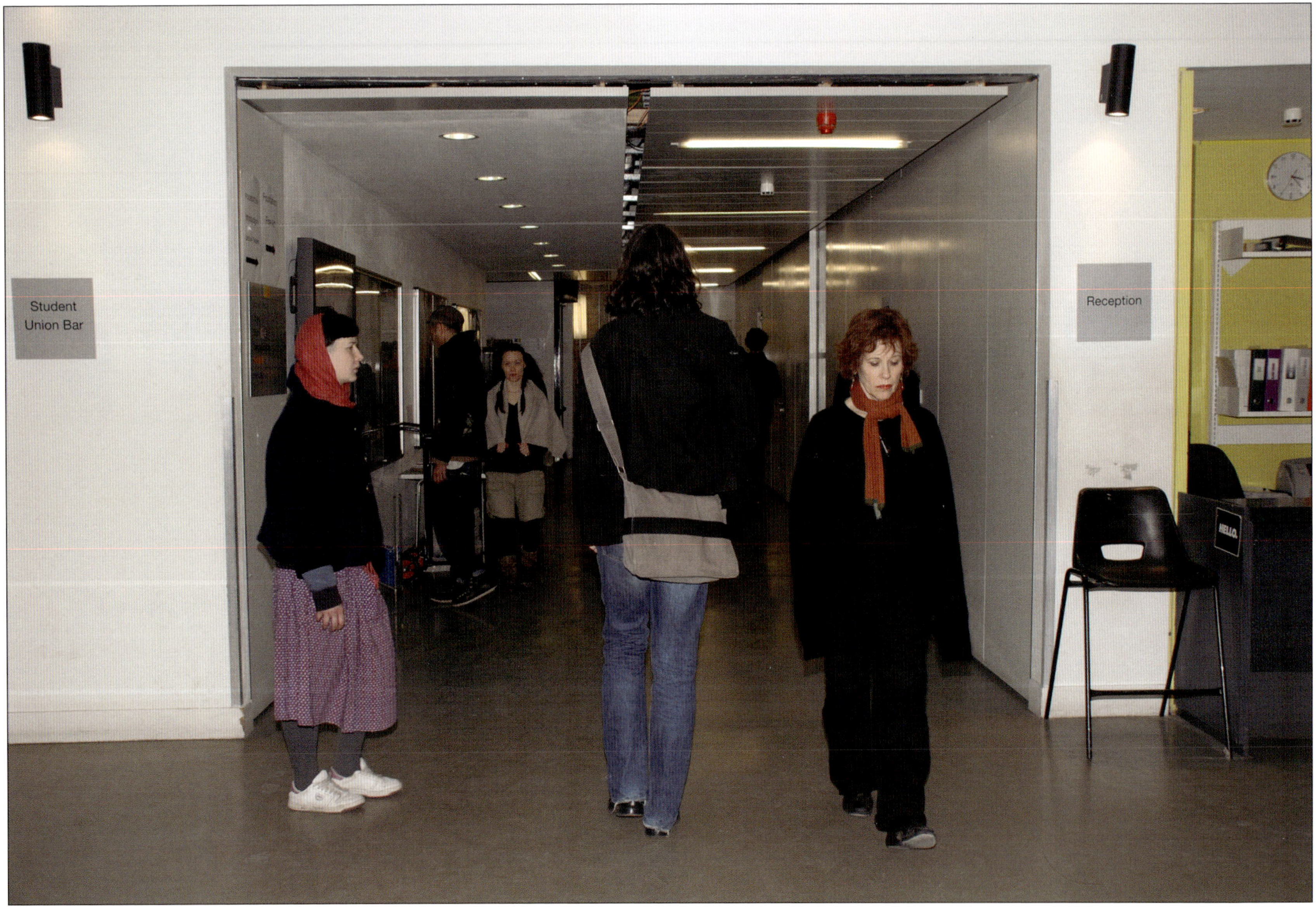

Walking Indoors. Chelsea College of Art and Design, London. 17 February 2010. Photo: Betty Borthwick

An added perspective comes from Peter Boardman in *The Shining Mountain* (1978): "Life has many cruel subtleties that require far more courage to deal with than the obvious dangers of climbing." What I'm engaged in feels extremely difficult. I don't mean the walking – I mean, linking – art – to – walking. The bringing together of two entirely separate activities. I'm not even sure if there's an audience for this kind of thing.
In 2002, I made an exhibition at the Tate in London. Seven years later, I summited Everest. Perhaps, a unique combination. But none of this has reduced the struggle. I'm no grand master of walking art: I'm a survivor with a *wealth* of walking experiences.
This artist's book is not only about a 21-day walk in the Cairngorms region of Scotland – it is also about a context surrounding the walk. I view the experience of walking as the connecting point for a wide range of topics. I'm an artist who walks, not a walker who makes art.

WALKING IS AN ART FORM IN ITS OWN RIGHT.

I think in phrases, statements (see bottom of page 77), not well-argued paragraphs. Inter-connections and/or **non sequiturs**? RANGZEN = Independence. Freedom and justice for the people and land of Tibet.
My daily practise is to write in notebooks (see pages 14, 70, 75) – pen on paper. Every day – at home, travelling (trains, airports) or on a walk. Although I say walking is an art form in its own right, so far, this fact has not been widely considered. In identifying myself as a 'walking artist' (no mention of a traditional art medium) I also state that I'm not a landscape artist. Would a landscape artist make indoor walks (see opposite page)? It seems there are only two possibilities for 'landscape art': (carbon dioxide) paintings from the past (also painted today, in the styles of the past) and outdoor sculpture in the present. Author Rebecca Solnit (*Wanderlust: A History of*

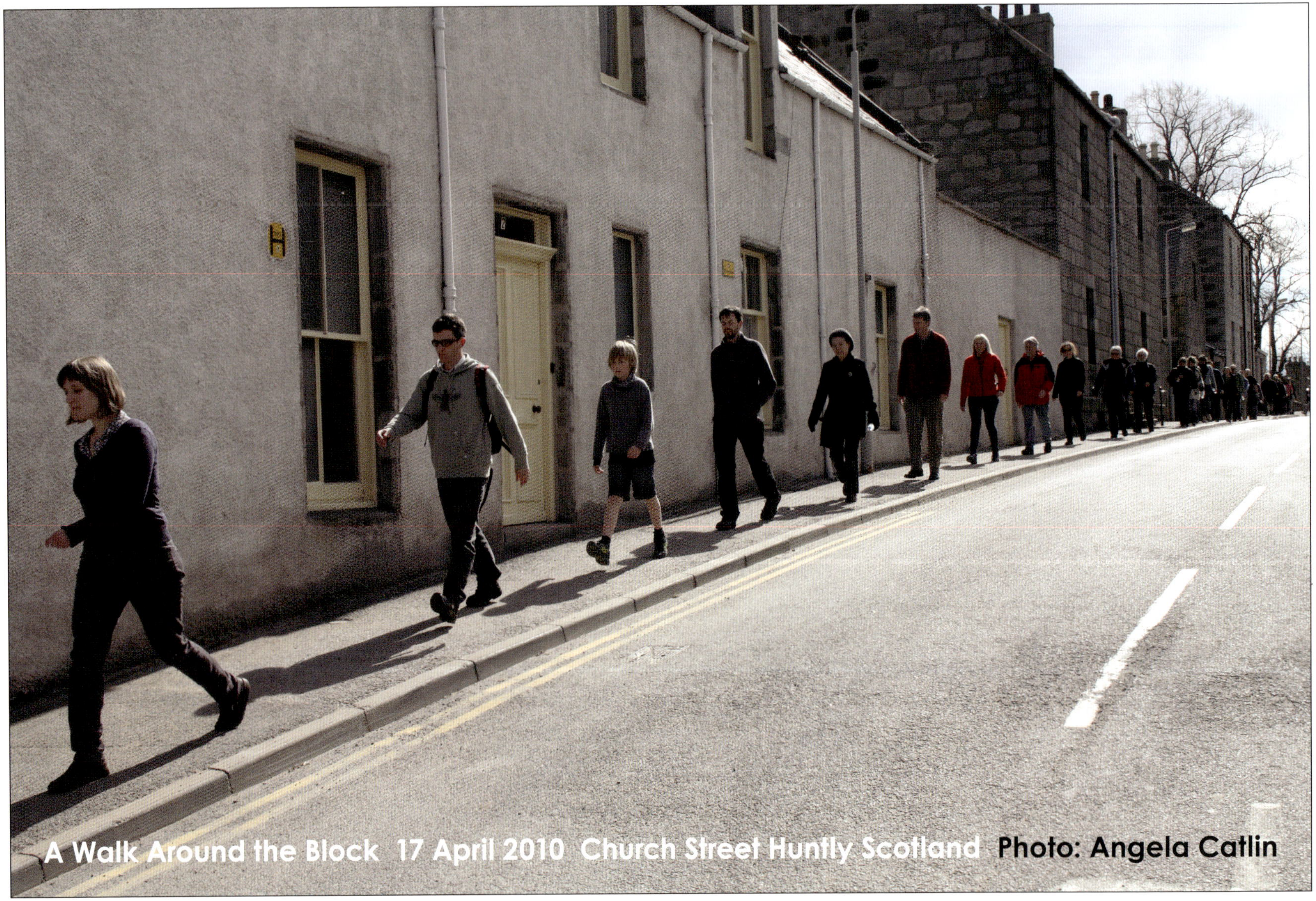

A Walk Around the Block 17 April 2010 Church Street Huntly Scotland Photo: Angela Catlin

Walking, 2000) cites Lucy Lippard in tracing "the parentage of walking as a fine art to sculpture, not performance." No mention of any opposition between Land Art and the North American ethical practise of **Leave No Trace** (or L.N.T. see: N.O.L.S, National Outdoor Leadership School). I chose a Jim Crumley quote with L.N.T. in mind: "the dismantling of every man-made artefact in the mountains." Dotterel, Heather, Capercaillie, Juniper, Blaeberry, Osprey, Golden Eagle.

In considering the differences between sculpture and walking, I have for some years been making urban group walks (see opposite page). Group artwalks use what is already there – public pavements. Except for the experience, nothing is *built*. Urban artwalks exist in comparison to all other pedestrian activity. For the duration of an artwalk each participant is also an observer (see: Turner Contemporary. A walk in Margate for 198 people).

At the invitation of Claudia Zeiske at Deveron Arts (Deveron, name of the river) I made a group walk in Huntly, Scotland (Huntly has a population of about 4000).

A WALK AROUND THE BLOCK

33 PEOPLE ATTEMPTING TO WALK EQUI-SPACED IN SILENCE ROUND AND ROUND CLOCKWISE FOR TWO HOURS
ON THE PAVEMENTS OF: DUKE STREET MCDONALD STREET PROVOST STREET AND CHURCH STREET
HUNTLY ABERDEENSHIRE SCOTLAND SATURDAY 17 APRIL 2010

Members of the public accepted an invitation from Deveron Arts to join the walk, no set number of walkers required. Freedom inside the rules. Very simple rules. The facing forwards line of 33 walkers should be equi-spaced (maintaining throughout the two hours a constant space of

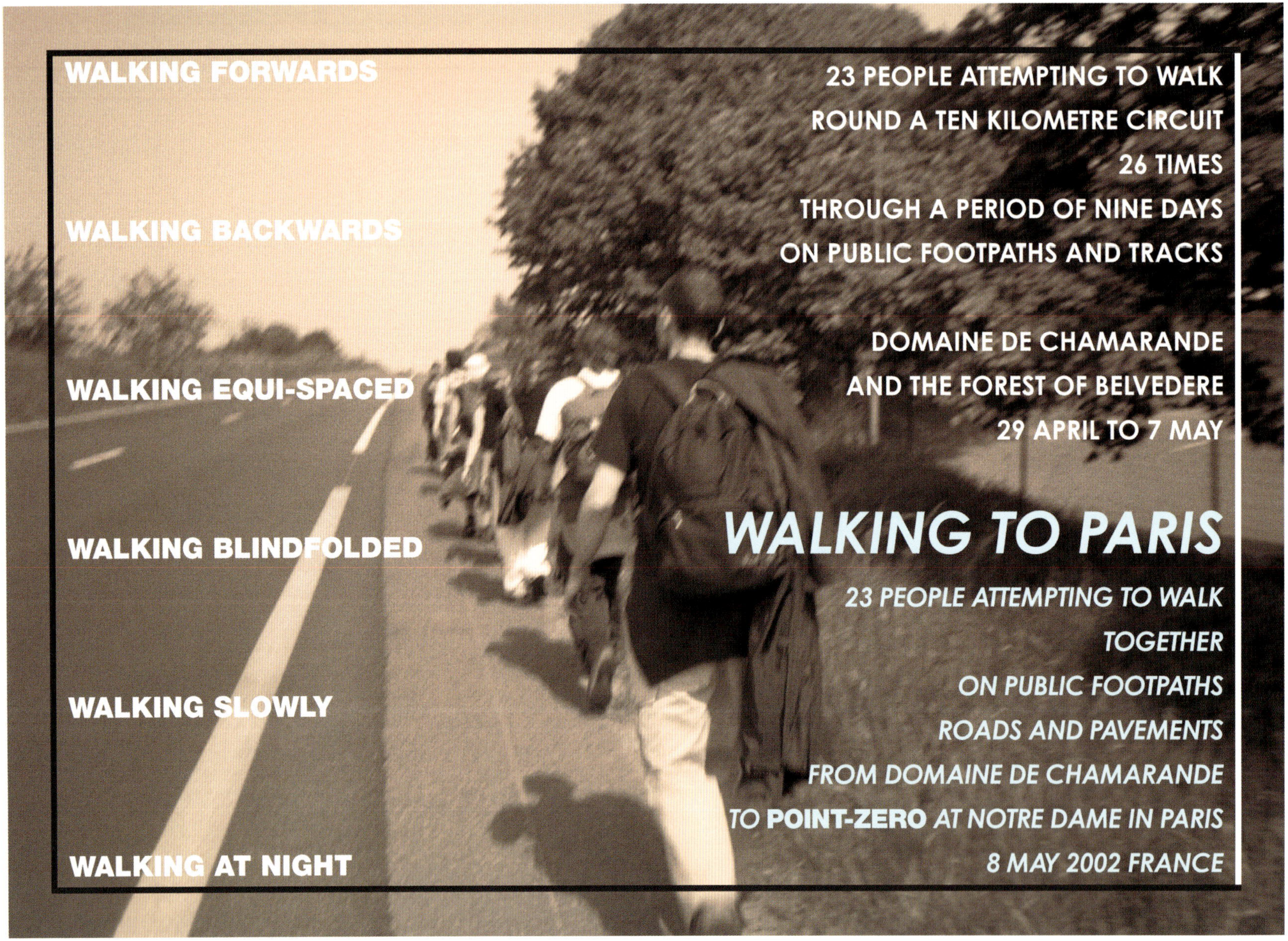

Hamish Fulton: Walking to Paris – Limited edition print and exhibition announcement card for Romain Torri, Paris, 2010

about two metres between "your toes and the next person's heels"). All in silence. No talking – just concentrate on the walk (mobile phones to be used only as clocks). In my walk text – my resulting art – I use the word *attempting*. The plan, the intention, was to walk equi-spaced in silence. This was not achieved by everyone. The person directly in front of me caught up to the person in front of them and started a conversation. Simple instructions, but difficult for those people who are unfamiliar with or do not like this category of walking (an opposite of hill walking). "I'd sooner walk two miles over a hill than one mile down a road." I'm in a different position – I'm the author of these walks and I participate in every one of them. Besides saying that: "the time passed quicker than I would have expected" – that "the experience was meditative and communal" – members of the public are sometimes of two minds as to whether the walk was interesting or boring. This combined response I think is *creative*. The Huntly walk was executed "on-sight" – with no practise time. Whereas, for the nine days of walks at Chamarande in 2002 there were opportunities to practice the various walks (see opposite page). After completing my 21-day walk from Huntly Square to Glenmore Lodge (Glenmore Lodge is the Scottish National Outdoor Training Centre) I made a second group walk also organized by Deveron Arts – deliberately located at Aviemore Ski Car Park. Meditative and another opposite of hill walking.

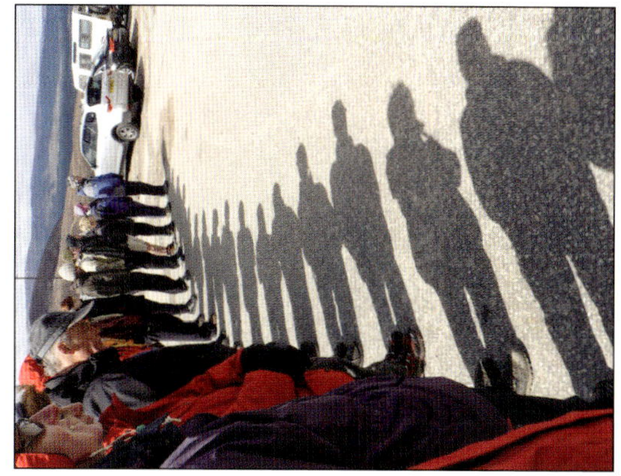

Slowalk Photo: Peter Moore

SLOWALK 28 PEOPLE WALKING A DISTANCE OF THREE METRES
SIDE BY SIDE IN SILENCE FOR THE DURATION OF ONE HOUR
AVIEMORE SKI CAR PARK CAIRNGORMS SCOTLAND 9 MAY 2010

For my 21-day walk, Deveron Arts had organised a group of generous walkers to accompany me for the first day. A unique experience, to set off with what might be termed a support group. My usual anonymous E & E (entrance and exit) is a platform at Aviemore station (night trains from London).

In September 1996 I attempted to walk round Mýrdalsjökull, an icecap in southern Iceland. South of Porsmork, I tried to ford the river. Unfortunately at that time, it was too deep and too fast, so I had to retrace my steps.

I'd packed the rucksack for a twenty-one-day walk. Returning back round to the start, the experience transformed into a fourteen-day walk – resulting in double-day rations for the last week. "Don't give up, try again." I returned in June 2008 (see opposite page) to "try again". Second time lucky, a normal river crossing, then south on the Brattafönn trail between Mýrdalsjökull and Eyjafjallajökull.

14 April 2010, Eyjafjallajökull erupted causing widespread disruption to air travel. Worldwide, an estimated ten million passengers were unable to travel. 16 April, the day I should have flown from London to Aberdeen, all flights were grounded (the sounds of passenger jets subtracted from the environment).

'Uncontrolled' nature reminds us that it still has the power to disrupt our very recent reliance on technology. The root cause of global warming is our lack of respect for every form of life, except our own. Our industrial systems do not acknowledge the diversity of life forms. When we take measures to reduce (or avoid) the effects of increased temperatures we are thinking only of our own preservation. (Rebranding. Is China's concern with a new low-carbon economy so that it can dominate the new technologies?) Same day, 14 April 2010, a lesser known 'news story' on the other side of the world, an earthquake in Tibet killed 2,700 people and left 100,000 homeless.

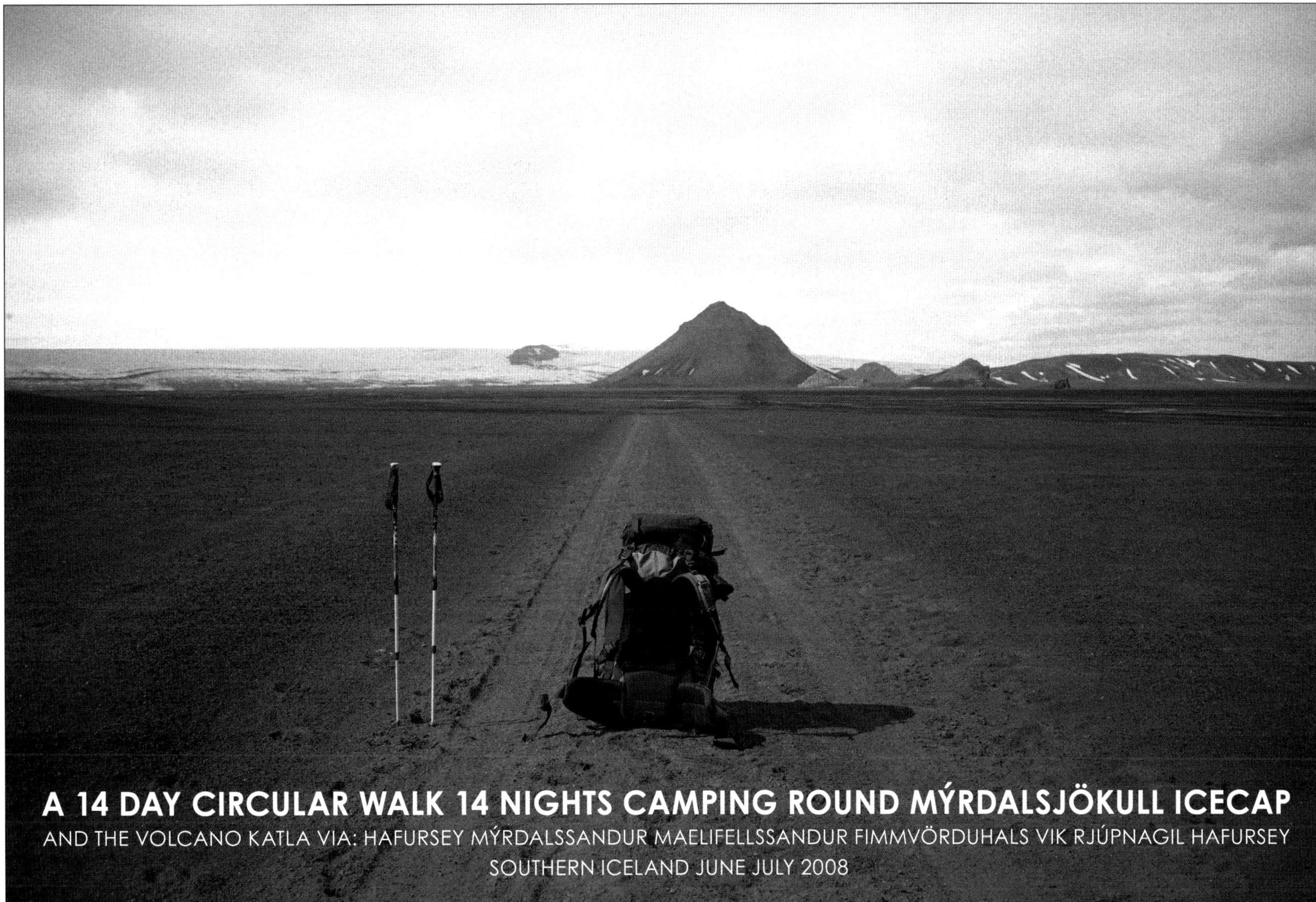
A 14 DAY CIRCULAR WALK 14 NIGHTS CAMPING ROUND MÝRDALSJÖKULL ICECAP
AND THE VOLCANO KATLA VIA: HAFURSEY MÝRDALSSANDUR MAELIFELLSSANDUR FIMMVÖRDUHALS VIK RJÚPNAGIL HAFURSEY
SOUTHERN ICELAND JUNE JULY 2008

I, by comparison, had purposely left my home, to camp out for twenty nights. Having been to Tibet, I know that the Tibetan people already live in a 'Chinese prison'. For the people to suffer again in this way is a tragedy beyond comprehension. Will the rebuilding of Tibetan homes be in line with traditional Tibetan design?

According to Adam Watson, a highly respected authority on the Cairngorms, the name 'Cairngorms' is only a nickname. The correct title is: Am Monadh Ruadh, meaning the red-hill range. The massif is small, an area of only 30 kilometres east to west and 25 kilometres from north to south.

For my walk (carrying everything for 21 days in the one rucksack) from Huntly Square, it took some time to arrive in what I would call the true Cairngorms. Before arriving at the top of Ben Avon (bain' aan) in a whiteout, I took what is considered to be an unappealing route to Glen Builg. For me, road walking is one of the things I do; I enjoy all forms of walking (colliding tests).

As a total experience, this was a walk of a lifetime. A walk of great luck (there is focus and skill, and there is also luck). It was an easy walk over a short distance. Sometimes, the time is right.

The days leading up to departure had been, as usual, hectic and stressful. Treadmilling impossible schedules. I no longer purchase specialist dehydrated food (no Gu gel). Instead I buy cheap supermarket food. Every day the same – 50 grams of breakfast cereal, 50 grams of dried fruit, nuts and chocolate for lunch. Soup for dinner. No shortage of hot sweet drinks. (The Dee and Spey are reported to be the cleanest rivers in Scotland). When I unpacked my rucksack at the first night's camp (45 minutes spent trying to find a dry area for my tent) – I saw a 'picture' of my stressed but experienced mind – that had chosen, assembled and been able to pack everything into one rucksack. The pack I chose was a Crux AK70 (70 litres). The trick was to get everything inside, nothing on the outside, exposed to the elements. For what was essentially a winter walk – I prefer to use a spacious tent. I did not take my Mountain Hardware Solitude, much smaller and consequently occupying less space in the rucksack. Instead I packed my Terra Nova Voyager (a seven-letter word). Providing much more 'elbow room' and only 300g heavier (see pages 71, 72, 74). So far, nothing new here for generations of hill walkers – except perhaps for the length of continuous camping time devoted to so few walked miles. To walk my same route in one third of the time would miss the point and be of no interest to me (see pages 8, 9).

MY IDEA WAS TO SLOW DOWN – AND LIVE CLOSE TO NATURE, TO RECEIVE INFLUENCES FROM NATURE.

3 August 1989 I walked into a Harvard Square bookstore and found *The Rights of Nature* by Roderick Nash (also published in 1989). Today, 2010, this important reference book is considered to be standard material in most U.S. universities. As an artist, *The Rights of Nature* has had a profound influence on my thinking and practice, making the 'Angel of the North' an impossibility.

Although form, colour, scale, weight and surface texture are the characteristics of every thing, they are not high on my art priority list. Neither is cynicism. Scepticism, yes. After several years of attempts, Galleri Riis in Oslo was able to arrange a meeting for me with the great Norwegian philosopher and mountaineer Arne Naess (organised with the help of one of his former students). Sunshine and blue skies. Snow covered ground in the outer suburbs of Oslo. We knock at the door, 12 March 2005. Arne greets us and I extend my hand to shake his – which he transforms into a bout of arm wrestling. This 'breaking of the ice' was followed by laughter and Gandhian Boxing! I purchased my first book about/by Arne Naess on 26 June 1993 – after: A FOURTEEN DAY WALK FOURTEEN NIGHTS CAMPING TETON RANGE WYOMING USA EARLY SUMMER 1993 (see pages 14, 15). I had brought with me this same worn copy of *Is It Painful To Think?* (conversations with Arne Naess and David Rothenberg). I asked Arne if he could autograph the book, which he kindly agreed to, adding the word 'sometimes' next to the title. Why did I want to meet Arne Naess? In fact, for many reasons (including his playfulness) but certainly I was attracted to his

GERONIMO

WALKING FOR 16 DAYS CAMPING FOR 16 NIGHTS

GUIDED BY THE AVAILABILITY OF WATER DURING A DROUGHT YEAR

1 2 3 4 5 6 7 8

VIA THE HEADWATERS OF THE GILA RIVER

HOMELAND OF GERONIMO

AND THE WORLDS FIRST DESIGNATED WILDERNESS AREA

HOMELAND

NEW MEXICO U.S.A. WANING MOON OF MAY 2006

9 10 11 12 13 14 15 16

famous phrase "Simple in means, rich in ends".
Naess joined the word ecology (a seven-letter word) to philosophy, producing: Ecosophy.
Arne Naess also gave the world: Deep Ecology. "Shallow ecology, he believed, meant thinking the big ecological problems could be resolved within industrial capitalist society." (Walter Schwarz, *The Guardian,* 15 January 2009). Arne Naess died in his sleep – 12 January 2009 – at the age of 96. (see: YouTube, The Call of the Mountain, Arne Naess).
(29 January 2009 – I made a group walk in Canterbury, England, with 39 participants.)
In May 2006, with the help of Fredericka Hunter, I visited the Gila wilderness in New Mexico (see page 48). The Gila is where Geronimo (the patriot) was born and where Aldo Leopold (a seven-letter name) was able to create the world's first designated wilderness area. *Silent Spring* (1962) by Rachel Carson and *A Sand Country Almanac* (1949) by Aldo Leopold form the cornerstones of modern environmental studies. In his chapter titled THINKING LIKE A MOUNTAIN, after the shooting of a wolf (the last wolf in Scotland was killed around 1743) Leopold reflects: "We reached the old wolf in time to watch a fierce green fire dying in her eyes. I realized then, and have known ever since, that there was something new to me in those eyes – something known only to her and to the mountain. I was young then, and full of trigger-itch; I thought that because fewer wolves meant more deer, that no wolves would mean a hunters' paradise. But after seeing the green fire die, I sensed that neither the wolf nor the mountain agreed with such a view."
Compared with the country John Muir walked through in the U.S., the Cairngorms are very small and not very wild. This makes the case for their preservation all the more poignant. Threatened biodiversity. "I think wild land as a resource is undervalued. It is not well protected or placed on a priority list." Robert McMoran, Research Associate at the Centre for Mountain Studies in Perth, Scotland. The Cairngorms are the most extensive area of subarctic landscape in Britain – they are the

highest, wildest, coldest, snowiest. (Shelter for all forms of life can be found down in the trees – Caledonian Pine.)
My title for this publication is MOUNTAIN TIME HUMAN TIME. These four words are constructed with 21 letters – 21 letters for a 21-day walk. "THINKING LIKE A MOUNTAIN" is also assembled with 21 letters… as is PRESERVATION OF THE WILD and DRINKING FROM MOUNTAINS.
Mountains, the great givers of life, providers of water. *Respect the mountain respect the river.*

SEVENTH – WALKING IS A SEVEN-LETTER WORD

Seven, the readymade – the seventh wave, the seven colours of a rainbow. Rainbow is a seven-letter word. Uses for the number 7 already exist in the world – the trick is to discover them.
I made my first seven-day walk in the Cairngorms twenty-five years ago. Unlike a walking journey where the number of days is open – "it will take as long as it takes". A totally different system is to set the number of days to be walked in advance. The duration of the walk is therefore determined by a number, not terrain or weather. (Weather is a seven letter word.)
After completing 7 x seven-day walks (1985–1991) I made an eighth walk – necessitating continuing to 14 x seven-day walks. In 2002 I made a fourteen-day walk in the Cairngorms. In 2004 I set in motion a further round – by making my fifteenth seven-day walk. This year, 2010 – (seven days, fourteen days and now) a twenty-one-day walk. (Total: 140 days.) Question: into the same Crux rucksack must go everything – for a future (as yet unmade) twenty-eight-day walk (see page 62)? Food, smaller and smaller. Rucksack, same size.
The one walk I've made that combines various rules is my 21-day road walk on France, from the Mediterranean Sea to the north coast – starting on the first day of June – with the (calculated) plan of arriving (at the next sea) on the day of the summer solstice. The solstice – (not mid-

summer's day) being on the twenty-first day of the month (see page 58). This walk was about 600 miles longer than my Cairngorms 21-day walk.

To date, I have made nine 21-day walks (see page 64). By far the wildest was in the Wrangell Saint Elias Region of Alaska (1999). This trek was re-supplied and I was accompanied by an alpine guide (see page 61). My wildest solo walk was in the Beartooth Mountains of Montana 1997 (see page 60). My best cultural 21-day walk was in Japan (1996). During which, almost by surprise I found myself (camping beside a busy main road) in Ueno – birthplace in 1644 of Matsuo Basho – Japan's greatest Haiku poet (see pages 33, 34). Basho was born at the time of the September full moon (see page 60).

What on **Earth** is all this about? I attempt to link art and walking. Walking can compare and connect urban life (half the world's population live in cities) with nature, wild nature. "Nature will survive, but wild nature may not." Gary Snyder, U.S. poet. (see: Carolyn Merchant, *The Death of Nature*, 1980.) As I write this, the U.K. government is planning to sell off nature reserves, rivers, forests. Perhaps David Cameron should read Wallace Stegner's 1960 *Wilderness Letter*.

At the top of the 2010 list, the most important is wild nature.

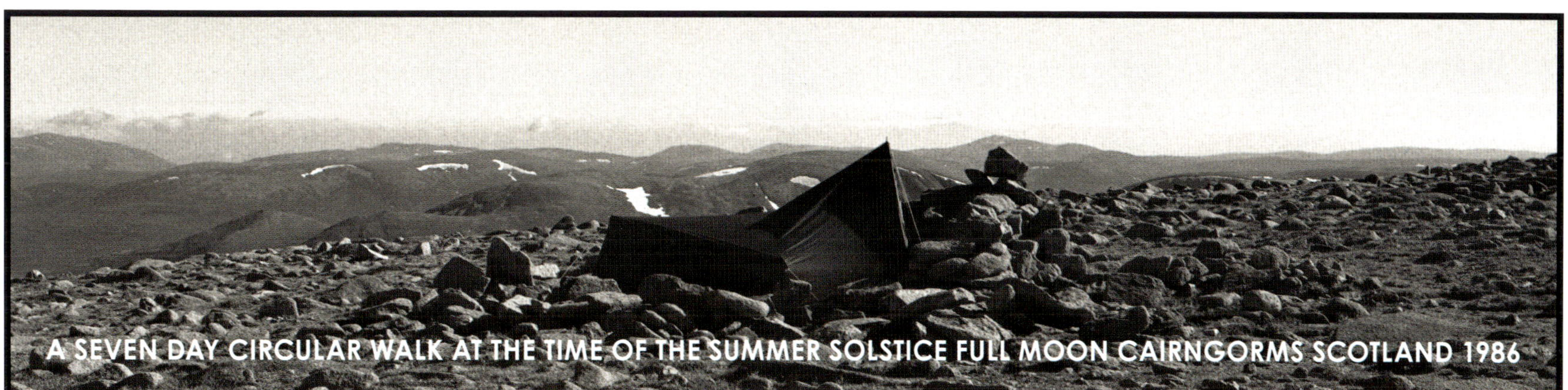

A SEVEN DAY CIRCULAR WALK AT THE TIME OF THE SUMMER SOLSTICE FULL MOON CAIRNGORMS SCOTLAND 1986

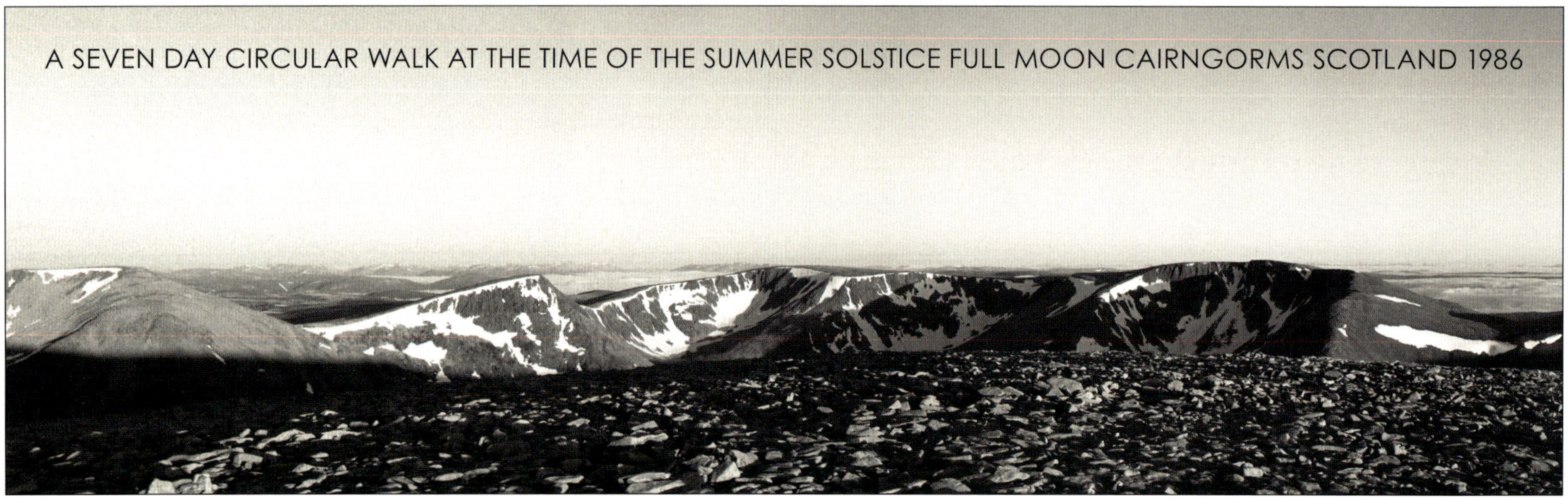
A SEVEN DAY CIRCULAR WALK AT THE TIME OF THE SUMMER SOLSTICE FULL MOON CAIRNGORMS SCOTLAND 1986

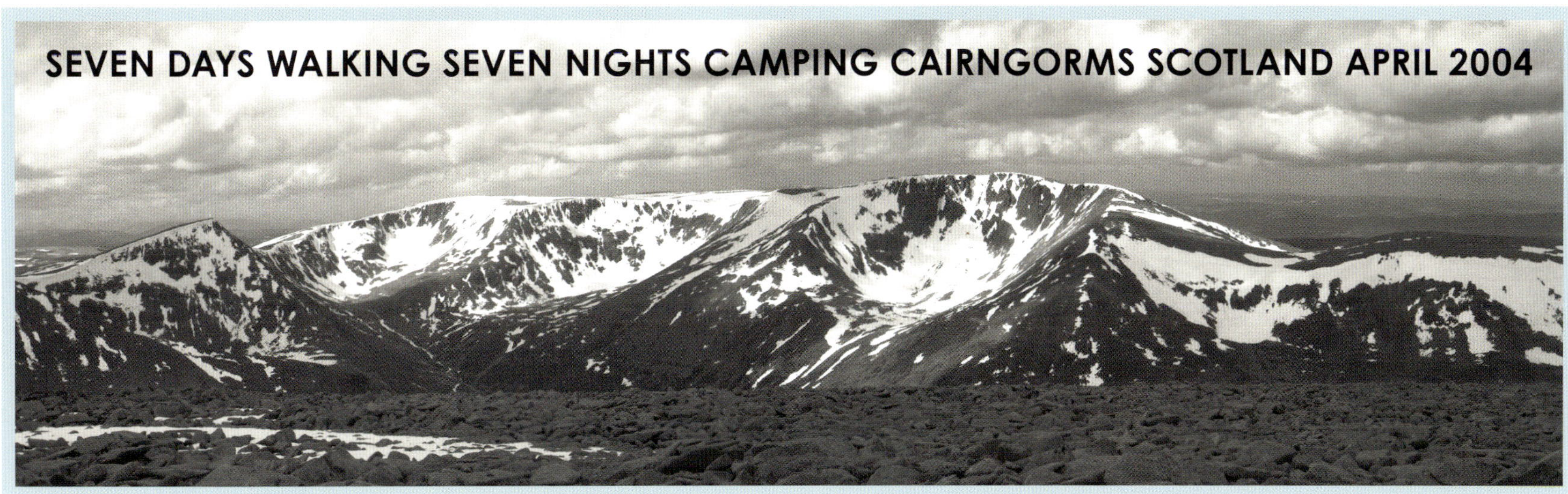
SEVEN DAYS WALKING SEVEN NIGHTS CAMPING CAIRNGORMS SCOTLAND APRIL 2004

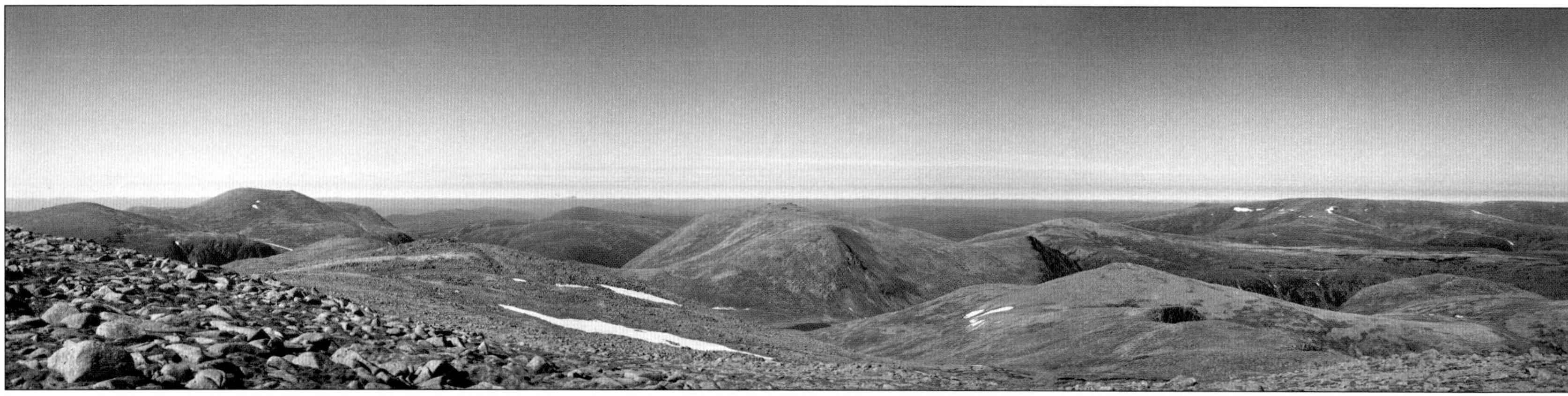

A SEVEN DAY CIRCULAR WALK AT THE TIME OF THE SUMMER SOLSTICE FULL MOON CAIRNGORMS SCOTLAND 1986

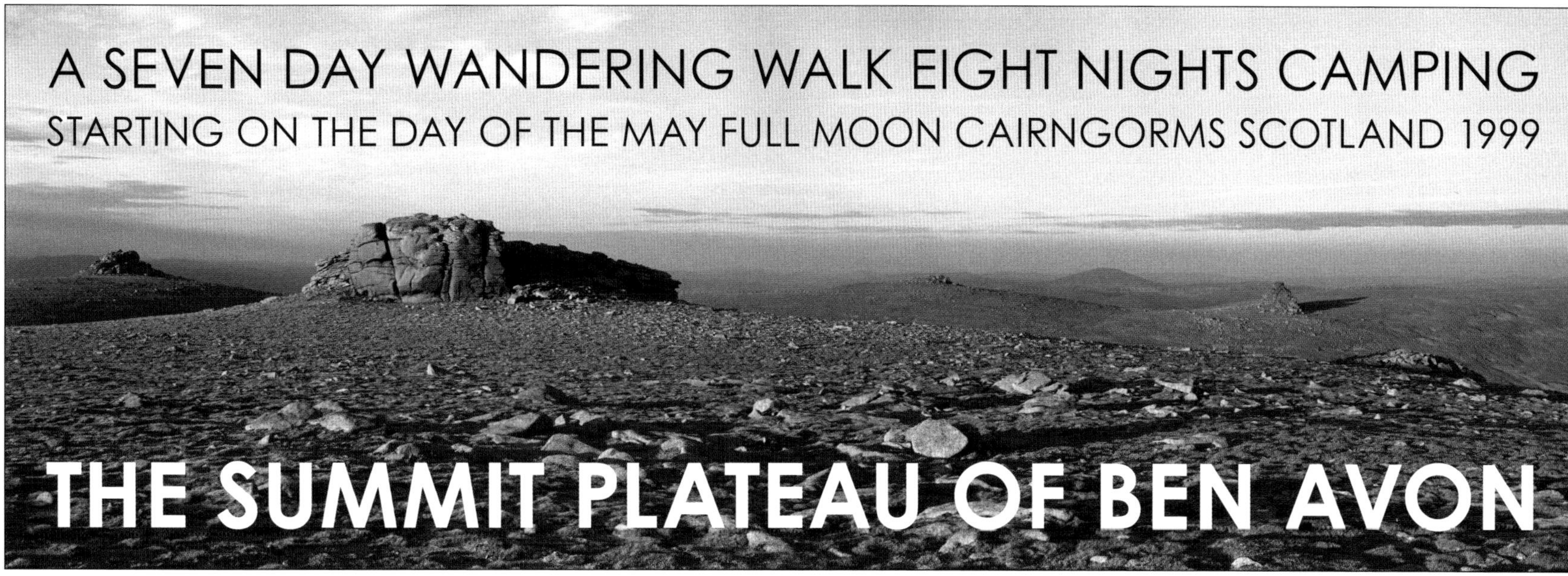
A SEVEN DAY WANDERING WALK EIGHT NIGHTS CAMPING
STARTING ON THE DAY OF THE MAY FULL MOON CAIRNGORMS SCOTLAND 1999
THE SUMMIT PLATEAU OF BEN AVON

NO TALKING FOR SEVEN DAYS

WALKING FOR SEVEN DAYS IN A WOOD
CAIRNGORMS SCOTLAND
FEBRUARY FULL MOON 1988

SEVEN

ONE DAY WALKS

ON HIKOSAN

OUT AND BACK

ENDING

AT THE TIME

OF THE FIRST

FULL MOON

OF MARCH 1999

KYUSHU

JAPAN

SEVEN

DAYS WALKING

SEVEN

NIGHTS CAMPING

ENDING

AT THE TIME

OF THE SECOND

FULL MOON

OF MARCH 1999

CAIRNGORM MOUNTAINS

SCOTLAND

FROM
COAST
TO
COAST
A LINE
BETWEEN
THE MORNING SUN
AND
THE EVENING SUN
A ROAD WALKING JOURNEY
FROM THE MEDITERRANEAN SEA TO THE ENGLISH CHANNEL
NARBONNE-PLAGE TO BOULOGNE-SUR-MER
FRANCE 1–21 JUNE 1992

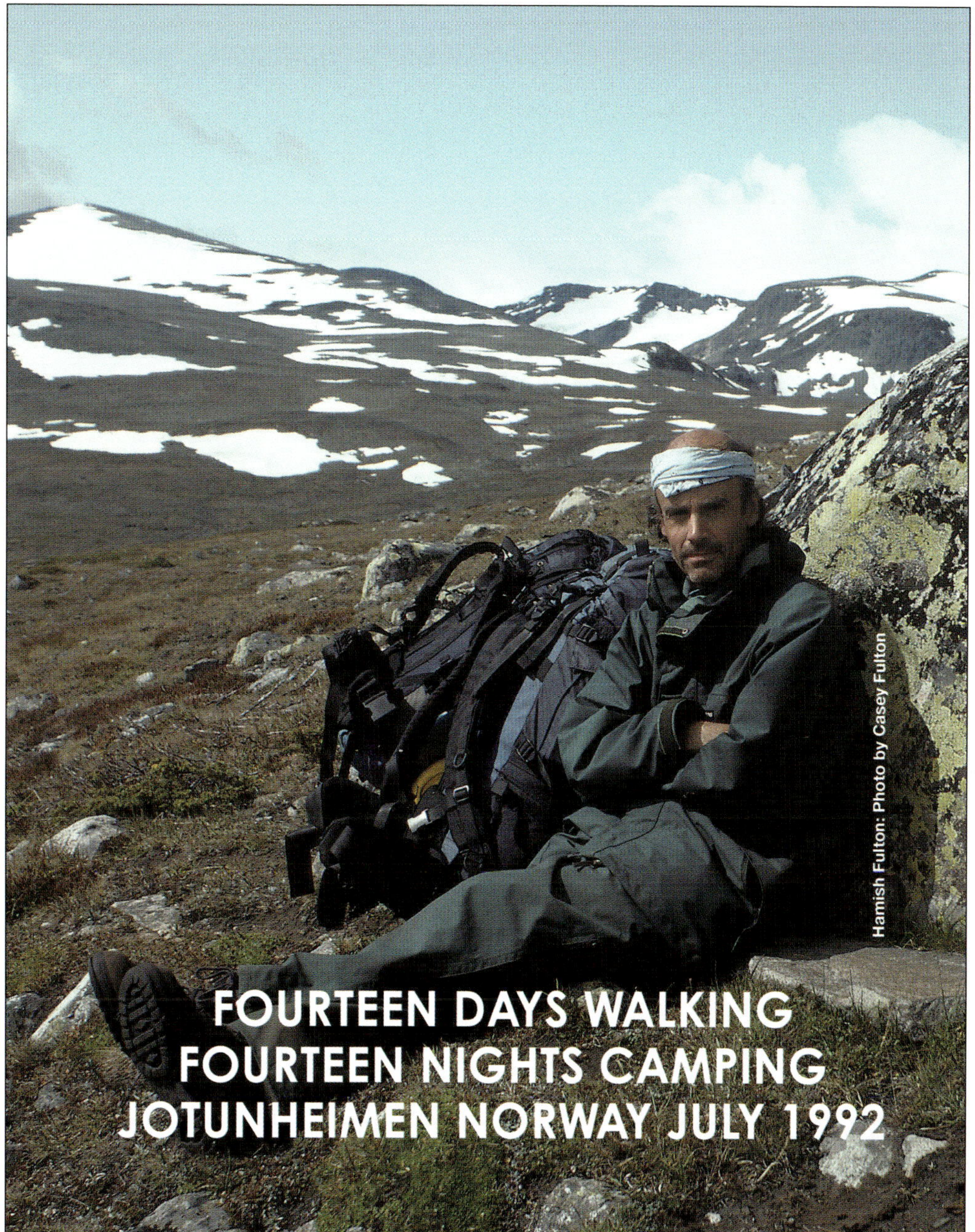
FOURTEEN DAYS WALKING
FOURTEEN NIGHTS CAMPING
JOTUNHEIMEN NORWAY JULY 1992
Hamish Fulton: Photo by Casey Fulton

A 21 DAY WANDERING WALK 20 NIGHTS CAMPING IN THE BEARTOOTH MOUNTAINS OF MONTANA ENDING WITH THE SEPTEMBER FULL MOON 1997

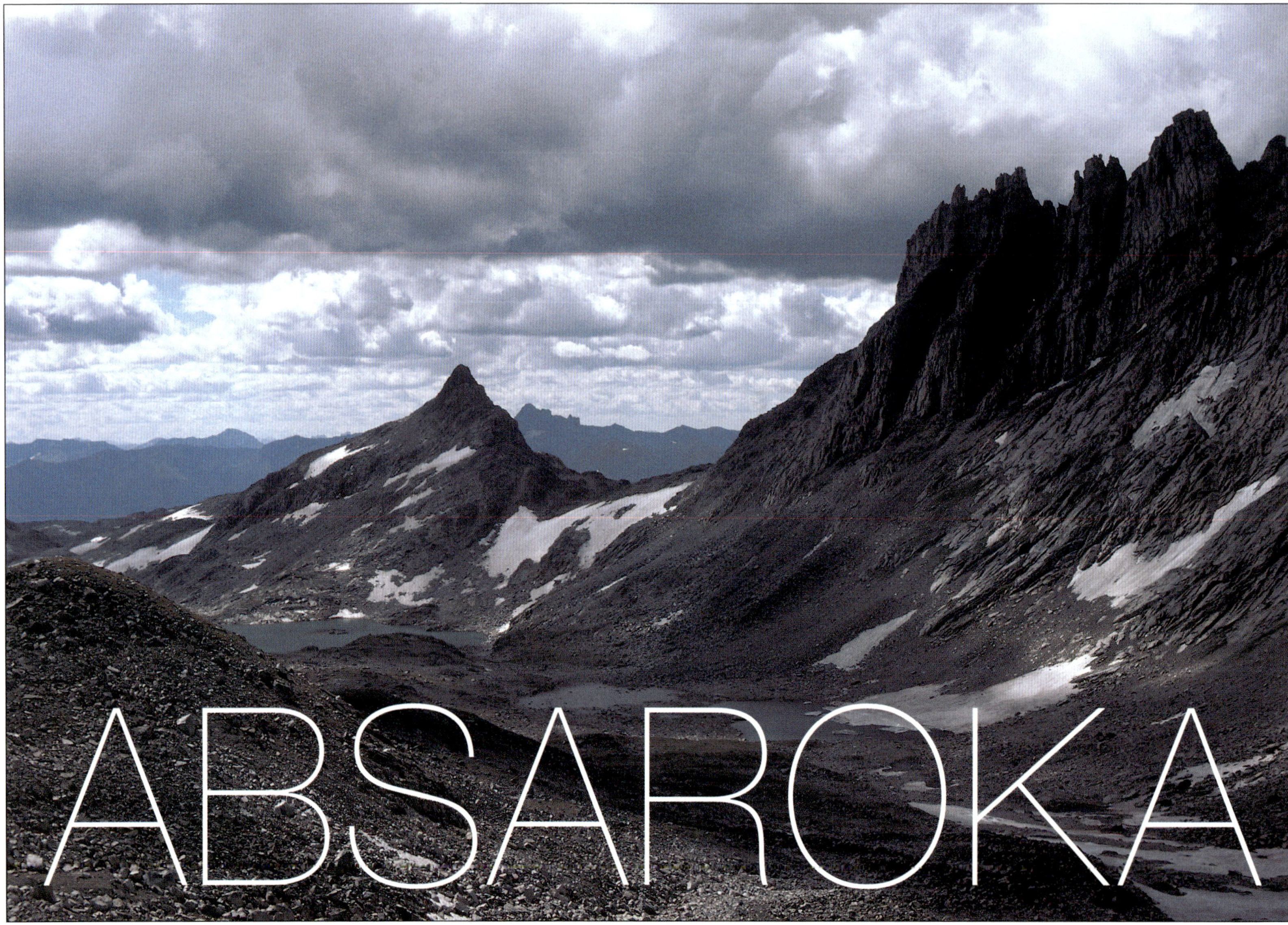

A 21 DAY CROSS COUNTRY WALKING JOURNEY GUIDED AND RESUPPLIED IN THE WRANGELL SAINT ELIAS REGION OF ALASKA LATE SUMMER 1999

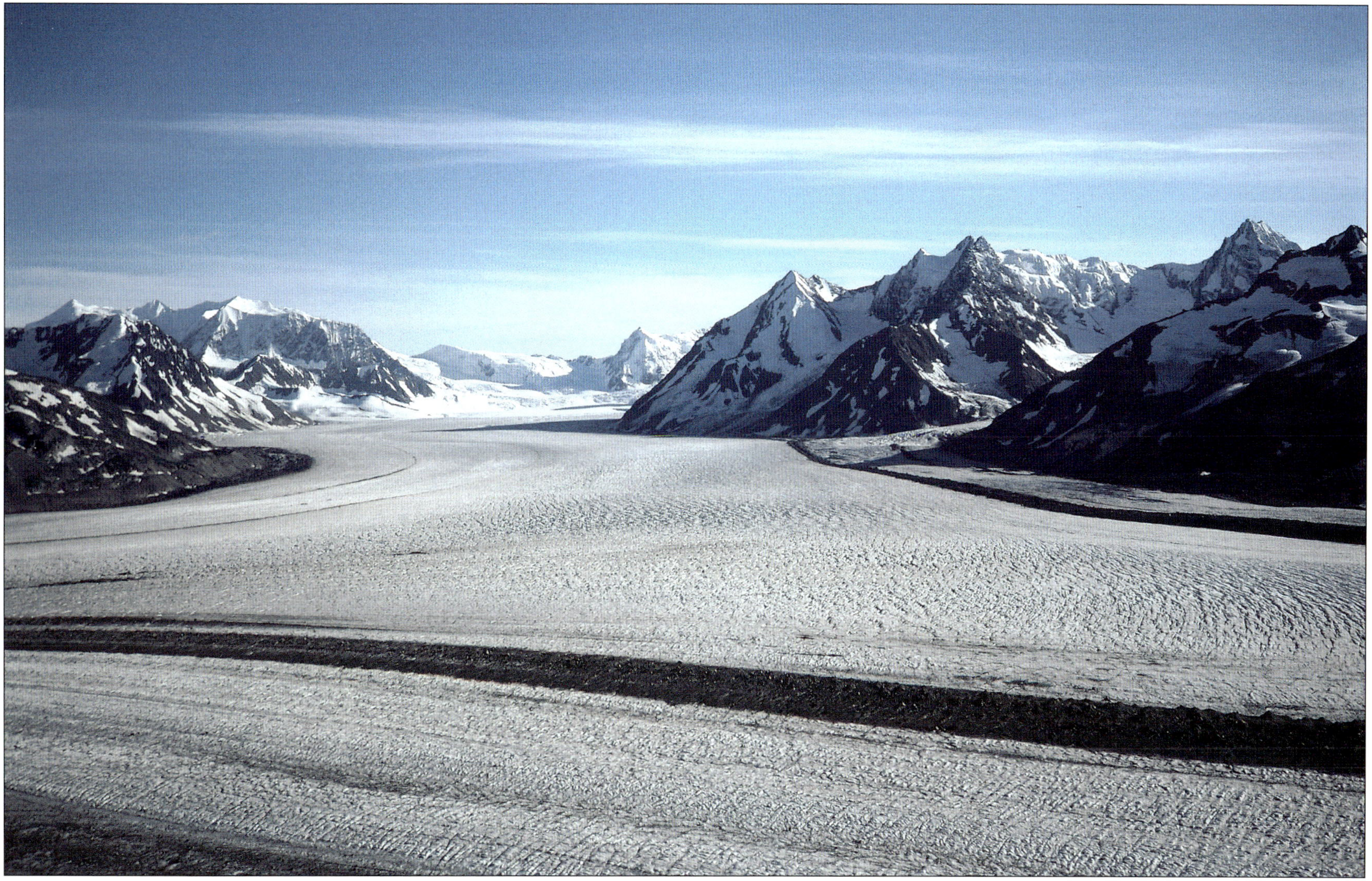

7

7 JORNADAS DE CAMINATA A TRAVÉS DE LA CUMBRE DEL MULHACÉN
SIERRA NEVADA ESPAÑA INVIERNO 1992

14

UN VIAJE A PIE DE 14 DÍAS
POR CARRETERAS Y CAMINOS
DESDE LA COSTA ATLÁNTICA HASTA ARRIBA EN LAS MONTAÑAS
Y VOLVER A BAJAR HASTA EL BORDE DE LAS AGUAS
NORTE DE ESPAÑA FINALES DEL VERANO 1993

21

UN VIAJE A PIE DE 21 DÍAS POR CARRETERA
DESDE LA COSTA NORTE A LA COSTA SUR DE ESPAÑA
DE RIBADESELLA A MÁLAGA INVIERNO 1990

28

UN VIAJE A PIE DE 28 DÍAS POR CARRETERA
DESDE LA COSTA SUR A LA COSTA NORTE DE ESPAÑA
PARTIENDO DE LA DESEMBOCADURA DEL RÍO GUADALQUIVIR
EN EL GOLFO DE CÁDIZ
ACABANDO EN LA DESEMBOCADURA DEL RÍO NERVIÓN CERCA DE BILBAO
17 SEPTIEMBRE – 14 OCTUBRE 2003

A TWENTY ONE DAY CIRCULAR ROAD WALK IN EXTREMADURA

FROM AND TO THE RIVER GUADIANA AT BADAJOZ

VIA GUADALUPE COUNTING FORTY NINE BAREFOOT PACES ON A STONE PAVEMENT

FOR THE FORTY NINTH YEAR OF THE DALAI LAMA'S EXILE

DURING THE NIGHT OF THE JANUARY FULL MOON

SPAIN EIGHTH YEAR OF THE TWENTY FIRST CENTURY

NINE 21 DAY WALKS

A 21 DAY COAST TO COAST ROAD WALKING JOURNEY FROM SOUTH WALES TO NORTH EAST ENGLAND BY WAY OF SEVEN HILL TOPS LATE SUMMER 1987 BRECON BEACONS CADER IDRIS BLEAKLOW HEAD CLEVELAND HILLS YORKSHIRE DALES HELVELLYN CHEVIOT HILLS

A 21 DAY ROAD WALKING JOURNEY FROM THE NORTH COAST TO THE SOUTH COAST OF SPAIN WINTER 1990

A ROAD WALKING JOUNREY FROM THE MEDITERRANEAN SEA TO THE ENGLISH CHANNEL NARBONNE-PLAGE TO BOULOGNE-SUR-MER FRANCE 1–21 JUNE 1992

A 21 DAY COAST TO COAST WALKING JOURNEY ON ROADS AND PATHS STARTING ON THE FIRST DAY OF MAY FROM THE MOUTH OF THE KAMENO RIVER IN WAKAYAMA ENDING AT THE MOUTH OF THE MIYA RIVER IS ISE TRAVELLING BY WAY OF SHIONOMISAKI KUMANO HONGU SHAKAGATAKE OMINE MIWASAN MOUNT HIEI MIUNE YAMA KII PENININSULA JAPAN 1996

A 21 DAY WANDERING WALK 20 NIGHTS CAMPING BEARTOOTH MOUNTAINS OF MONTANA U.S.A. ENDING WITH THE SEPTEMBER FULL MOON 1997

A 21 DAY CROSS-COUNTRY WALKING JOURNEY GUIDED AND RE-SUPPLIED IN THE WRANGELL SAINT ELIAS REGION OF ALASKA U.S.A. 1999

A 21 DAY WALKING JOURNEY ON PAVEMENTS BICYCLE PATHS TRACKS FOOTPATHS ROCKS AND SNOW STARTING BY ENCIRCLING OBERSEE AND ZÜRICHSEE 19 & 20 AUGUST CONTINUING TO THE TOPS OF SEVEN SMALL ENGADIN MOUNTAINS PIZ JULIER PIZ CORVATSCH PIZ DE LA MARGNA GREVASALVAS PIZ LANGUARD PIZ OT IGL COMPASS ENDING BY WALKING IN THE OPPOSITE DIRECTION ROUND OBERSEE AND ZÜRICHSEE 7 & 8 SEPTEMBER SWITZERLAND SEVENTH YEAR OF THE TWENTY FIRST CENTURY

A 21 DAY CIRCULAR ROAD WALK IN EXTREMADURA FROM AND TO THE RIVER GUADIANA AT BADAJOZ VIA GUADALUPE COUNTING FORTY NINE BAREFOOT PACES ON A STONE PAVEMENT FOR THE FORTY NINTH YEAR OF THE DALAI LAMA'S EXILE DURING THE NIGHT OF THE JANUARY FULL MOON SPAIN EIGHTH YEAR OF THE TWENTY FIRST CENTURY

A 21 DAY WALK 20 NIGHTS CAMPING FROM HUNTLY SQUARE TO GLENMORE LODGE VIA: BEN AVON SGÒR GAOITH EINICH CAIRN BRAERIACH BEN MACDUI BEINN MHEADHOIN BYNACH MORE THE CAIRNGORMS REGION OF SCOTLAND 18 APRIL – 8 MAY 2010

WALKING

1 2 3 4 5 6 7

FOURTEEN DAYS WALKING FOURTEEN NIGHTS CAMPING CAIRNGORMS SCOTLAND EARLY 2002

CAMPING

8 9 10 11 12 13 14

THE THING TO BE KNOWN by Jim Crumley

THE MEANING

The plateau narrows to half a mile,
a neck atop shoulders. Beyond
the neck, the hoary skull of Am Braigh Riabhach.
Braigh is prosaic—"summit"; but
an old Gaelic dictionary has a poet's thesaurus
stashed away against Riabhach:
"drab, greyish, brindled, grizzled".

Sit awhile beside this haunt of the eternal miracle.

Look at it.

Listen to it.

Taste it.

You will never encounter anything like it, unless you come back and sit here again, so once you have looked and listened and tasted, look around and remember where you are. Remember where the miracle unfolds.

No, it doesn't unfold, does it? It bursts. But it bursts gently, gently but also irresistibly. You could no more confine its gentle energy than you could catch Niagara in a bucket.

You did well to choose today to see it, for often it does not appear as itself. Sometimes you cannot see it at all, not hear it, and obviously, in those circumstances you cannot taste it either. Yet it is still where it always is, unseen, unheard, untasted, still miraculous. Sometimes the ice seems to confine it. Yet something, some sinuous string of water, must still move beneath even the weightiest ice, for the moment the ice relents the welling has already begun. And listen, for its voice sings, and if you have an ear for music at all, if you can pick out one pitch from another, you hear many voices, like a far-off choir muffled by cathedral walls. Sometimes, if there is a weight of snow on the ice (a far from rare occurrence hereabouts), that seems to silence it. But it is only silent to your ears and mine. It is never silent within the mountain. Nor is it silent within itself, nor is it confined. It is always singing, it is always free.

Taste it again. It is so cold it is almost beyond taste, and yet far back in your throat and once the shock abates, you sense the unmistakable flavours of wilderness. Your life will never know anything purer than this.

This is what the word "elemental" means. This is an element at its source, before you or I or the rest of our tribe have had the chance to corrupt it, a raw, pure, primitive thing, and utterly, utterly baffling. Nan Shepherd, poet of these mountains, wrote:

Like all profound mysteries, it is so simple that it frightens me.

It is water. *Fuaran Dhe*, the Wells of Dee, 4000 feet, the summit plateau of drab, greyish, brindled, grizzled Braigh Riabhach. It wells and it springs. You look at it and you suddenly realise why wells are called wells and springs springs. They are not nouns at all—they are verbs. They were named after what they do. What wells here, what springs, is the River Dee. What astounds me, what will surely astound you, is that it gathers up its various wellings and springings and is at once river, fluent and fully formed, a 4000-feet-high river, a water-snake a-slither on the plateau. All it has to do now is grow.

I want to invent something that lets me see inside the mountain. I want to x-ray its ribcage and its vital organs to see how this works. I want to know how the river begins. No, I can see how the river begins, I want to know how the wells begin and what urges them to well, what galvanises the springs to spring. I want to know if there is a great chamber of water. Is the mountain hollow? I want to know how the mountain inhales the juices of clouds and fills itself, and I want to understand the workings of that infallible pump that wells and springs water out onto the plateau so that it makes a river of itself at once, without benefit of gorges, confluences, lochs, tributaries. It is itself and nothing else, a stupefying simplicity.

But the miracle of it is as short in duration as it is eternal in its execution, for the momentum generated by the welling and the springing is its own downfall. With all the unfettered space of the plateau and *Am Moine Mhor,* the Great Moss, at its disposal to the south, and the prospect of widening leisurely miles all the way to Glen Feshie, it chooses north-east instead, and after less than half of one leisured mile it cuts a groove in the rim of the Garbh Choire and jumps off. Geronimo! Aberdeen here we come.

Follow it as far as the rim, beyond which it becomes the Falls of Dee. Already it has forgotten about wells and springs. Instead, it falls. And it has a new voice, something more hoarse, more baritone than all that has gone before (though with what tongues it converses deep inside the mountain before the welling and the springing, I have trouble imagining).

There are days, too, when it even forgets how to fall. These are the days of big winds cramming up the Lairig Ghru then bending and fanning out mightily in to the yawn of the Garbh Choire, pouring into the mountain's open throat, and so nonchalantly flipping the Falls back up head over their own heels and drenching their own riverbanks in watery perpetual motion (a wheel-less water-wheel) that your marvelling mind is numbed at the scope and scale and the stupefying simplicity of the forces that stalk the face of this land.

But it's too soon for the Garbh Choire for me, for one still besotted by the well-springing miracle, still high on the adrenaline of the plateau and its eternally infant river, still gloriously baffled by the accumulating sensations of the drab, greyish, brindled, grizzled mountaintop. Such a plateau feels to me as if it has been hoisted up between two precipices. I only have geology's word for it that it has all been ground down from mightier ranges. Besides, all this is mighty enough for me. I have always felt that up here I linger under the sky rather than on top of the mountain, for it is more a place of space than hard rock. True, the Highlands are a spreadeagle of mountain shapes reaching into endless distance, and down is a place you left behind long, long ago, and at your feet the river sings and whispers of its changing worlds, the underworld for the overworld, the body of the mountain for the skin of the mountain. But there is so much more space than all that. On the plateau, my eyes are forever reaching up, grappling with eagle realms.

I have been cold here beyond any sense of cold I thought it was possible to feel. It is the work of the wind, that cold, and it is as lethal as avalanches. Climbing up out of Coire Garbhlach, kicking steps up a snow ramp through the headwall, out onto the Great Moss, meeting the wind there piling up blue waves of space, and shuddering under every layer of protective clothing I own, pounding away across the Moss on thin, frozen snow, every blade of grass sheathed in ice, wondering what it would be like today up at the Wells. I never found out. Halfway across the Moss the wind stopped me, then blew me over. I gave up the unequal struggle. I turned and ran before it, let it blow me up on to Carn Ban Mor from where I dived down the track for Achlean in Glen Feshie. I was back at the road before I began to thaw out. I never like being beaten back by the mountain weather, but nor do I hesitate when I recognise that I am out of my depth. The plateau wind that coats grass in ice and blows me over like a leaf in a gale... I have nothing to prove in that kind of company.

But I have been warm on the plateau too. There was one August day up at the Wells when the planet stood on its head and it was cool down in Strathspey, for all was cloud-girt below the belt of corries to which Braigh Riabhach hitches the bouldery pleats of its skirts, yet it stayed warm and still on the plateau where the sun held sway for fifteen hours. Summer here is unlike other definitions of summer in lesser landscapes. It is brief and traumatic, and grass and leaf and bud rush out and you learn to expect the unexpected.

Look there: in the first yard of welling water there is a flurry of activity that is not all water. Look—wings! Something is bathing there. It rises on its tail and turns so that its white breast is in the sunlight. It's a dipper. And this is the highest birdbath in Scotland. He stands for a moment, shakes himself free of a tiny shower of drops, then spreads his wings on the ground like a back garden blackbird sunning himself.

Why is he here? After all, the mountain is awash with hill burns, pools, gravelly shallows, all of them (I would imagine) offering richer feeding than this. Once I met a dipper on the frozen shore of Loch Coire an Lochain at 3300 feet in April and thought I had made a rare discovery. Now this. Dipper flight is enslaved to watercourses and there are none that link Loch Coire an Lochain and the Wells of Dee, so I guess it's not the same bird. But there are watery tendrils of Coire nan Clach (the casually named Stony Corrie) or Coire Bogha-Cloich that reach almost as high as the Wells, and a dipper might venture up one of these on a warm day that made high-flying effortless. It all suggests at the very least a sophisticated awareness of mountain weather and summit conditions, and of course, the knowledge that the highest bird bath in Scotland is here.

And on another day, look at this. There is a shape on the ground, not stone, not tussock, not moss, not lichen. It just blinked. So, it has an eye, a tiny black jet. That blink at least tells you which end is which, and once you know that, you can make sense of the shape. Above the eye is a skinny caterpillar of white, an eye-stripe, and above the eye-striped a black cap. West of the cap, a short stab of black bill, beneath the eye a tufty white cheek, a grey muffler, a white cummerbund, a swathe of peach; east of all that an ad hoc pattern of all these shades, the haute couture of dotterel, a male brooding eggs.

Now, do try this: turn round, close your eyes for ten seconds, open them, turn back, and try and find him again. Feel your eyes flounder among the stones and what passes for grasses at this height. Damn, he's gone. And then he snaps back into focus. He has been where you left him all the time, and all that has moved is the blink of his eye. It is not easy being a dotterel in the high Cairngorms, living among waves of space and shielding eggs from summer snows. So nature compensates with gifts of camouflage and that capacity for rock-stillness, these and a lifestyle as exceptional and uncompromising as its surroundings—polyandry. To make the most of the short season of insect plenty on the summits and plateaux and bare shoulders, the female dotterel must maximise her resources—eggs. Conventional practice won't do here. Brooding eggs and loyalty to one mate and one nest are wasteful of dotterel resources, so the tribe goes in for what science calls 'reverse courtship', which is not as painful as it sounds. She wears the bright clothes, takes several mates, lays in one nest after another, and he broods the eggs in the muted colours and the rock stillness. Matriarchy at 4000 feet.

Or... look at this, here where the old snow clings to a rim of the plateau, the last few feet of a corrie headwall. The meltwater oozes down into a thousand crannies. A tribe of stoics lives here, hooked up to the drip feed of the snows, plants as specialised and rare as dotterels, as the lands itself. Brook saxifrages trail across a handful of sodden inches, life so tentative you wonder why it bothers. But then, for a week or two of high summer, it thinks vertical and thrusts a small white flower an inch towards the sky. The fact that it must thrust up through new snow on a late-June afternoon does not deter its mission. Others, like the alpine willow herb, resort to stoloniferous techniques, that is they creep, and to assist the creeping they throw down the gauntlet of a new root every other creeping inch. A feeble stem on the skinny side of slender, wobbles up to a hooded, drooping pink flower. Here is where you find the first rank of nature's heroes.

On another day of high summer, in the July of 1923, Seton Gordon (the godfather of all of us who walk this way with a writer's eye turned on the landscape) narrated an extraordinary detail:

> *At just 3925 feet above sea level—I mention the height because one rarely finds ptarmigan nesting at so great an altitude—a ptarmigan flew on white wings from her shallow nest containing three eggs. These eggs were unusual in shape, for they were long, thin and rather pointed. An interesting sequel was the finding of the nest of the same bird with similar curiously shaped eggs in the summer of 1924 within a hundred yards of the same spot.*

It is part of his extraordinary account of the events of that summer. Snow had fallen well into June and he encountered the Braigh Riabhach plateau in early July with 'all the appearance of midwinter'. There was an iceberg on Loch Coire an Lochain, and he guessed it had been frozen across until mid-June. At the Wells of Dee,

> *The grass was brown, and lay close-pressed upon the ground as though a mountain torrent had passed over it. Not a bud showed upon the innumerable plants of the dwarf willow and the rosettes of the cushion pink were brown and apparently lifeless… One could walk above the Wells yet be unaware of their existence.*

Then after nine days of warm weather Seton Gordon returned and found the place under enchantment.

> *…an almost unbelievable change had been wrought on the earth…*

There was new grass two or three inches long, the dwarf willow was in full leaf and the pinks had leafed and budded. But…

> *Summer had come with a rush to the Cairngorms but a full month of precious warmth had been lost to the hills, and summer that year lasted no more than a fortnight, for on the 26th of July a bitter north-east wind with driving snow swept the plateau of the Wells.*

Seton Gordon haunts my footsteps in these mountains, and especially high on this plateau that encapsulates so much of what he held dear about the Cairngorms and articulated with such fluency. I am inclined to quote him to the mountain:

> *In the immense silences of these wild corries and dark rocks the spirit of the high and lonely places revealed herself, so that one felt the benign influence that has from time to time caused men to leave the society of their fellows and live on some remote surf-drenched isle—as St Cuthbert did on Farne—there to steep themselves in those spiritual influences that are hard to receive in the crowded hours of human life.*

How well I remember reading that for the first time, although it seems strange to me now that there was a time in my life when his 1924 masterpiece, *The Cairngorm Hills of Scotland*, was not a fixture in my bookshelves or a companion in my rucksack. I had never read anything quite like it. In the copious literature of the Cairngorms, there *is* nothing quite like it. That single sentence stands alongside a sentence from Gavin Maxwell's *Ring of Bright Water* in my mind, two encounters with the written word that stopped me in my tracks and put my feet on a different path towards a different life:

> *For I am convinced that man has suffered in his separation from the soil and the other living creatures of the world; the evolution of his intellect has outrun his needs as an animal, and as yet he must still, for security, look long at some portion of the earth as it was before he tampered with it.*

Sit here with me on the summit of the land, look long at this untampered-with portion of the earth, prepare for the spirit of the high and lonely places to reveal herself. My seat is a random choice but somewhere between the Wells and the Einich Cairn of Braigh Riabhach. I sit to be closer to the landscape, to be a boulder. I watch the mountain and the sky as the spirit of the high and lonely places wells to a thumping heartbeat. But what is it, this spirit, what was Seton Gordon getting at, the better part of ninety years ago?

I think it is a collaboration of landscape forces, of light, of weather, of space, the mingled chemistry of which creates a tangible presence of nature that demands a response in those who encounter it. Respect for the spirit is the first commandment of the wilderness, and its inviolability should be the first consideration of all those who would pronounce on the Cairngorms today. And it lingers most blatantly on the plateau. There is no mountain sensation to compare with its sweeping plain, its corner-to-corner skies, the restlessness of its air that can wash great freedoms through a receptive human mind in the manner of St Cuthbert's surf. The spirit tramples the land in its storms, clings to every rock and stem and leaf and berry as the ptarmigan feather clings to the blasted heather stem. The spirit forages with the golden eagle, the ptarmigan, the high daring of the dipper, the foolery of the dotterel; with the fox, deer, mountain hare, wren, crevice-hunting spider, creeping brook saxifrage. The spirit in its unique Cairngorms distillation is Arctic. It is hard, harsh, elemental, unluxurious, the garb of a landscape pared to the bone.

To be alone on the plateau, to sit boulder-still and let your mind range over all the Cairngorms landscapes of half a lifetime and all their weathers, to climb, as it were, through the landscapes of your mind anchored to a belay of unflinching granite, is to know finally the touch of the spirit. Reach down through the years from this bright plateau to dark pinewood winters when the sun slept for a week and high noons were indistinguishable from their dawns and dusks, and recognise the same exalted common denominator, their rootedness in the same mountain embrace, the touch of the same spirit. There is a uniformity of presence that attends every step of the way from Spey to Dee, and it is that uniformity, translated by Seton Gordon as "the spirit of the high and lonely places", that so dignifies and distinguishes all the Cairngorms, all their moods, all their heights and depths, all their landscapes.

I have sat here watching the sky change—change attitude, mood, colour, light, and ultimately, season. A greying cloud swelled and swerved from the west, lured it seemed by the very presence of the mountain. It reached Braigh Riabhach blackening and furious, flinging fast rain, draining the rock of its red sun-fire, cloaking the plateau in an array of chills, then bombarding it with hailstones. Finally and briefly it snowed. The dervish was done in ten minutes and raced on to torment some other boulder dweller, unlocking the sun again as it fled, and trailing a rainbow in its black wake.

I watched its furious, drunken dance stumble down and up the far side of the Lairig Ghru, flay Beinn MacDuibh, lurch on down Cairn Gorm's blind side, and blot out both mountains entirely. For a moment there was nothing east of the Lairig but a rainbow jiving on a black backcloth, while I bathed in my restored summer as I watched winter's pointed reminder, a guerrilla band unwilling to honour the terms of the ceasefire because the warring of the seasons was so much more stimulating than the peace.

The rest of that day shone and tingled with the wake of that small wintry epilogue—or was it a prologue? The plight of these mountains had been much on my mind, for the spirit of the high and lonely places is as fragile as it is unique, and there is much about what is happening to the Cairngorms today that is thoughtless and self-indulgent and apt to trample the spirit underfoot. My mood somehow aligned and identified itself with the storm cloud as some kind of visitation from the spirit of the high and lonely places, and I fashioned a meaning from its rainbow.

The red is the blaze at the tip of the tiny cladonia lichen, the flame of the spirit, rooted in granite.

The orange is the eye of the golden eagle, the vigilance of the wilderness patrolling the territory of the spirit.

The yellow is the bill of the whooper swan, Arctic anthem of the spirit.

The green is the pinewood, cloak of the spirit, an unbroken lineage ten thousand years back to the ice.

The blue is the summer watersheet of the osprey loch where a spark of the spirit was rekindled.

The indigo and violet are the dusk skies of autumn and winter.

Such is my rainbow. I wish my fellow man in this landscape the unquenchable tenacity of the cladonia, the vigilance and the tolerance and the predatory judgment of the golden eagle, the anthem of the wilderness in his ears, a cloak of hodden green to blunt the storms, the sanctuary of a calm watersheet at his journey's end, and to root his ambitions for wilderness not in terms of years but of millennia. I hope he will learn again what his forebears once knew when they lived closer to the land, closer to the animal state, closer to the spirit of the high and lonely places, which is to respect rather than resent that nature will always outshine him, the land always outlast him; to acknowledge that there is no pot of gold at the rainbow's end, only a piece of the wilderness which is in better heart than it was simply because the rainbow touched and blessed and danced on.

I first came to these mountains more than 40 years ago, which in terms of the mountains is nothing at all, but as I write this it amounts to two-thirds of my life thus far. I was lucky to grow up in Dundee, in the last street in town with fields on the other side of the road, fields that climbed to a low ridge from which I could look north to the Sidlaw Hills. These became my apprentice hills where I learned to get lost and find myself again, where I met hill birds and beasts and flowers and old boys with canvas packs whose ancient dubbined boots were the same colour as their faces. In time I was directed further north into the Angus Glens where the Dreish and Mayar and their kin lifted me up onto a mountain's horizon for the first time. It was there, one day in September, strolling hands-in-pooches, and all the world blue and gold and warm, that I saw far in the north a long line of white, and had a sense of a glimpse of the promised land, the fabled snow-in-summer Cairngorms.

This was the hill-going tradition into which I was born, a tradition in which the Cairngorms always provided the ultimate horizon, and by the time I was ready for them it felt as if they were already familiar. My love of them, like the Dee at the Wells, was born fully formed and began to grow from that love-at-first sight moment. It grows still, and as Nan Shepherd wrote, "love pursued with fervour is one of the roads to knowledge". She also wrote that "the thing to be known grows with the knowing", and that is possibly the single truest thing I have ever heard, the truest thing that anyone so helplessly in love with the Cairngorms will ever learn. So sit awhile beside this haunt of the eternal mountain, look at it, listen to it, taste it, but softly, and one at a time. That way you learn that love pursued with fervour, that road to knowledge that never ends, because the thing to be known grows with the knowing.

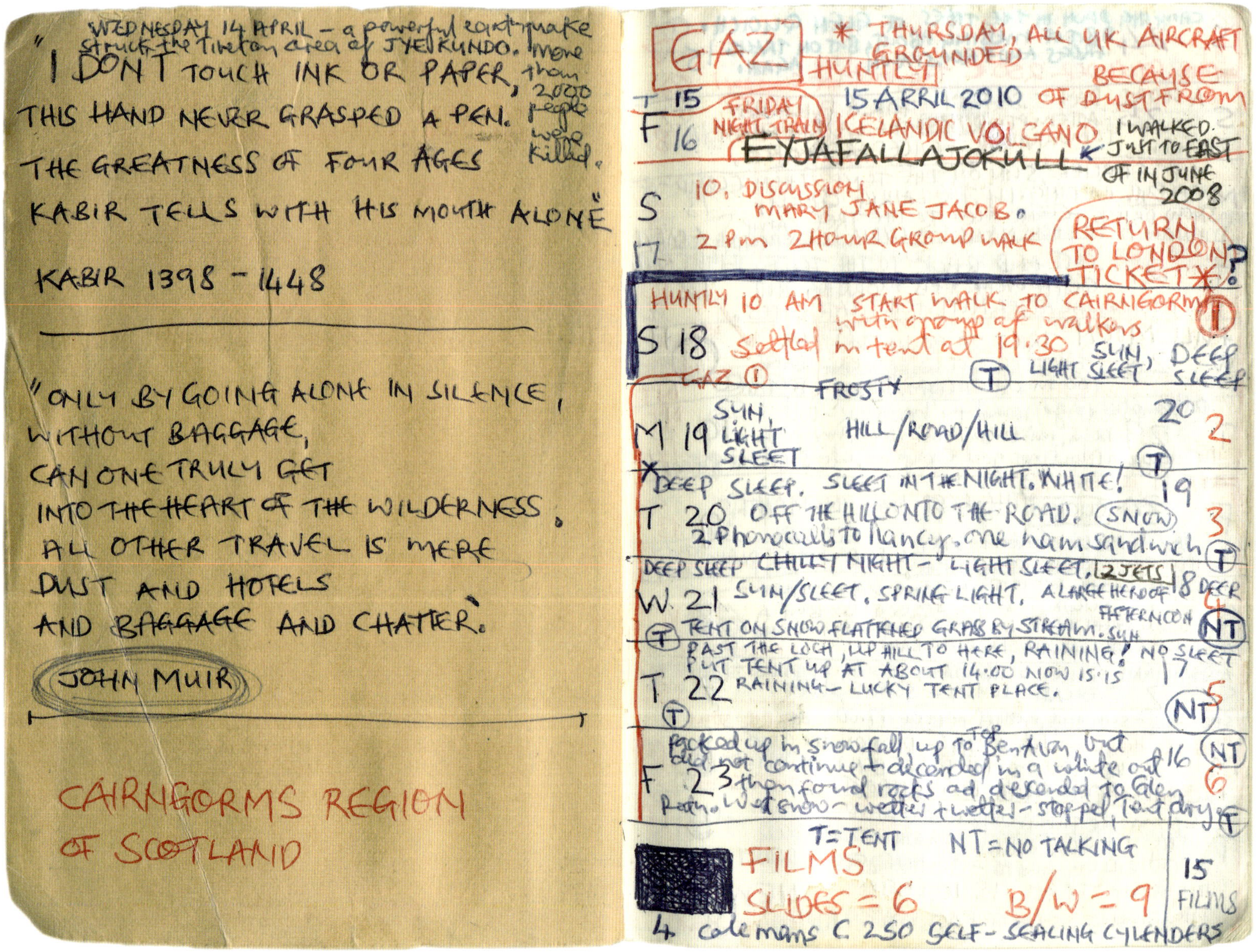
WEDNESDAY 14 APRIL – a powerful earthquake struck the Tibetan area of JYEKUNDO. more than 2000 people were killed.

"I DON'T TOUCH INK OR PAPER,
THIS HAND NEVER GRASPED A PEN.
THE GREATNESS OF FOUR AGES
KABIR TELLS WITH HIS MOUTH ALONE"

KABIR 1398 – 1448

"ONLY BY GOING ALONE IN SILENCE,
WITHOUT BAGGAGE,
CAN ONE TRULY GET
INTO THE HEART OF THE WILDERNESS.
ALL OTHER TRAVEL IS MERE
DUST AND HOTELS
AND BAGGAGE AND CHATTER."

JOHN MUIR

CAIRNGORMS REGION
OF SCOTLAND

GAZ
HUNTLY
* THURSDAY, ALL UK AIRCRAFT GROUNDED BECAUSE OF DUST FROM ICELANDIC VOLCANO
EYJAFALLAJOKULL ← I WALKED JUST TO EAST OF IN JUNE 2008

T 15
F 16 FRIDAY NIGHT TRAIN 15 APRIL 2010

S 17 10. DISCUSSION MARY JANE JACOB.
2 pm 2 HOUR GROUP WALK
RETURN TO LONDON TICKET *?

S 18 HUNTLY 10 AM START WALK TO CAIRNGORMS with group of walkers
Settled in tent at 19:30 SUN, LIGHT SLEET, DEEP SLEEP T

GAZ T FROSTY T
M 19 SUN, LIGHT SLEET HILL/ROAD/HILL 20 2 T

DEEP SLEEP. SLEET IN THE NIGHT. WHITE! 19
T 20 OFF THE HILL ONTO THE ROAD. (SNOW) 3
2 Phonecalls to Nancy. one ham sandwich T

DEEP SLEEP CHILLY NIGHT – LIGHT SLEET. 2 JETS 18 DEER
W 21 SUN/SLEET, SPRING LIGHT, A LARGE HERD OF AFTERNOON SUN 4 NT
T TENT ON SNOW FLATTENED GRASS BY STREAM.

PAST THE LOCH, UP HILL TO HERE, RAINING! NO SLEET 17
PUT TENT UP AT ABOUT 14:00 NOW 15:15
T 22 RAINING – LUCKY TENT PLACE. 5 NT
T

Packed up in snowfall up to top Ben Avon, but did not continue + decended in a white out 16 NT
F 23 then found rocks and descended to Glen Avon. Wet snow – wetter + wetter – stopped, tent dry. 6 T

T=TENT NT=NO TALKING
FILMS
SLIDES = 6 B/W = 9 15 FILMS
4 colemans C 250 SELF-SEALING CYLINDERS

Hamish Fulton. Cairngorms Diary, Spring 2010

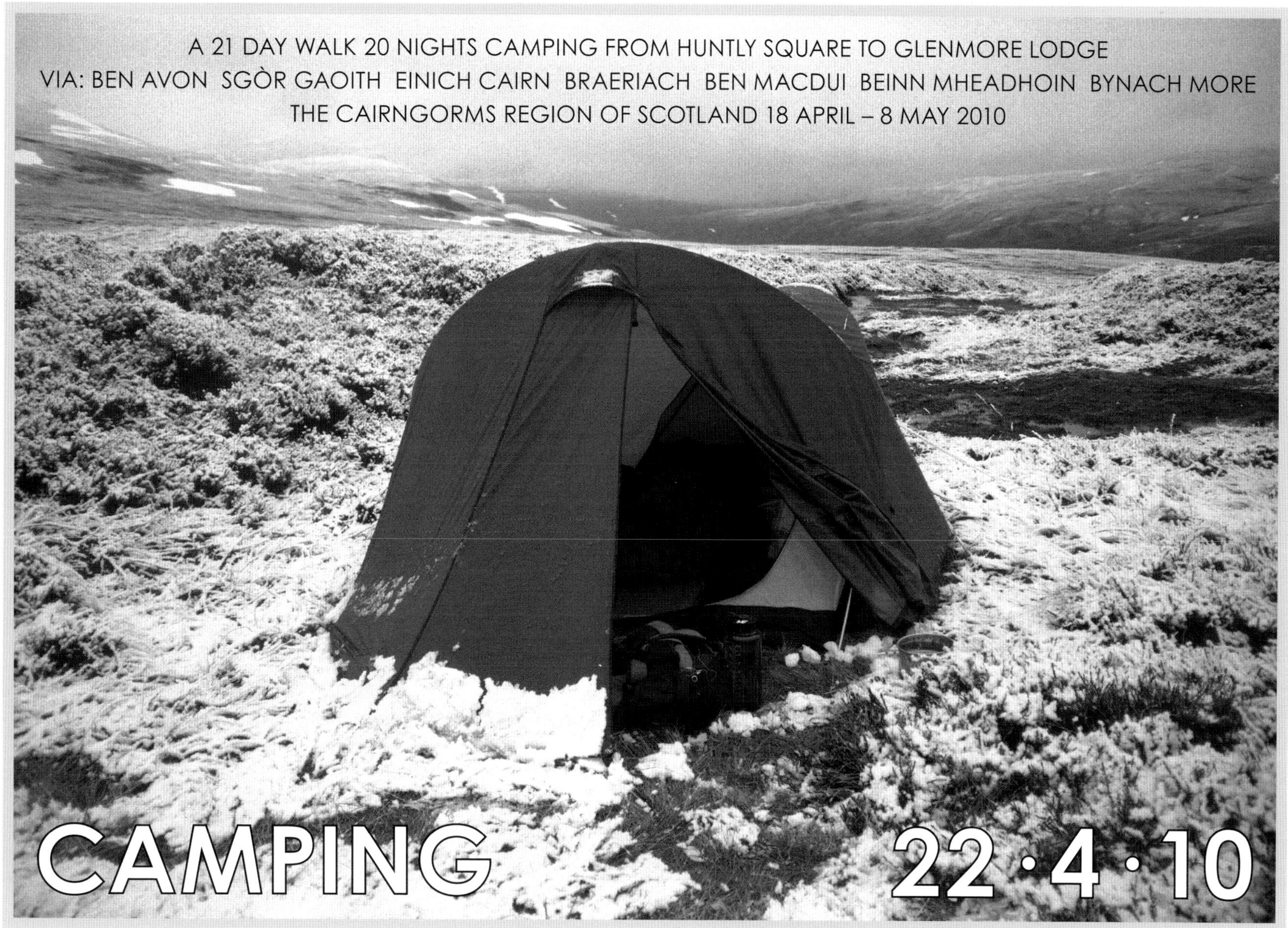
A 21 DAY WALK 20 NIGHTS CAMPING FROM HUNTLY SQUARE TO GLENMORE LODGE
VIA: BEN AVON SGÒR GAOITH EINICH CAIRN BRAERIACH BEN MACDUI BEINN MHEADHOIN BYNACH MORE
THE CAIRNGORMS REGION OF SCOTLAND 18 APRIL – 8 MAY 2010
CAMPING
22·4·10

Salomon Goretex walking boots.

Insulated drinking cup.

Stove.

Cooking pot.

Crux AK70 Rucksack.

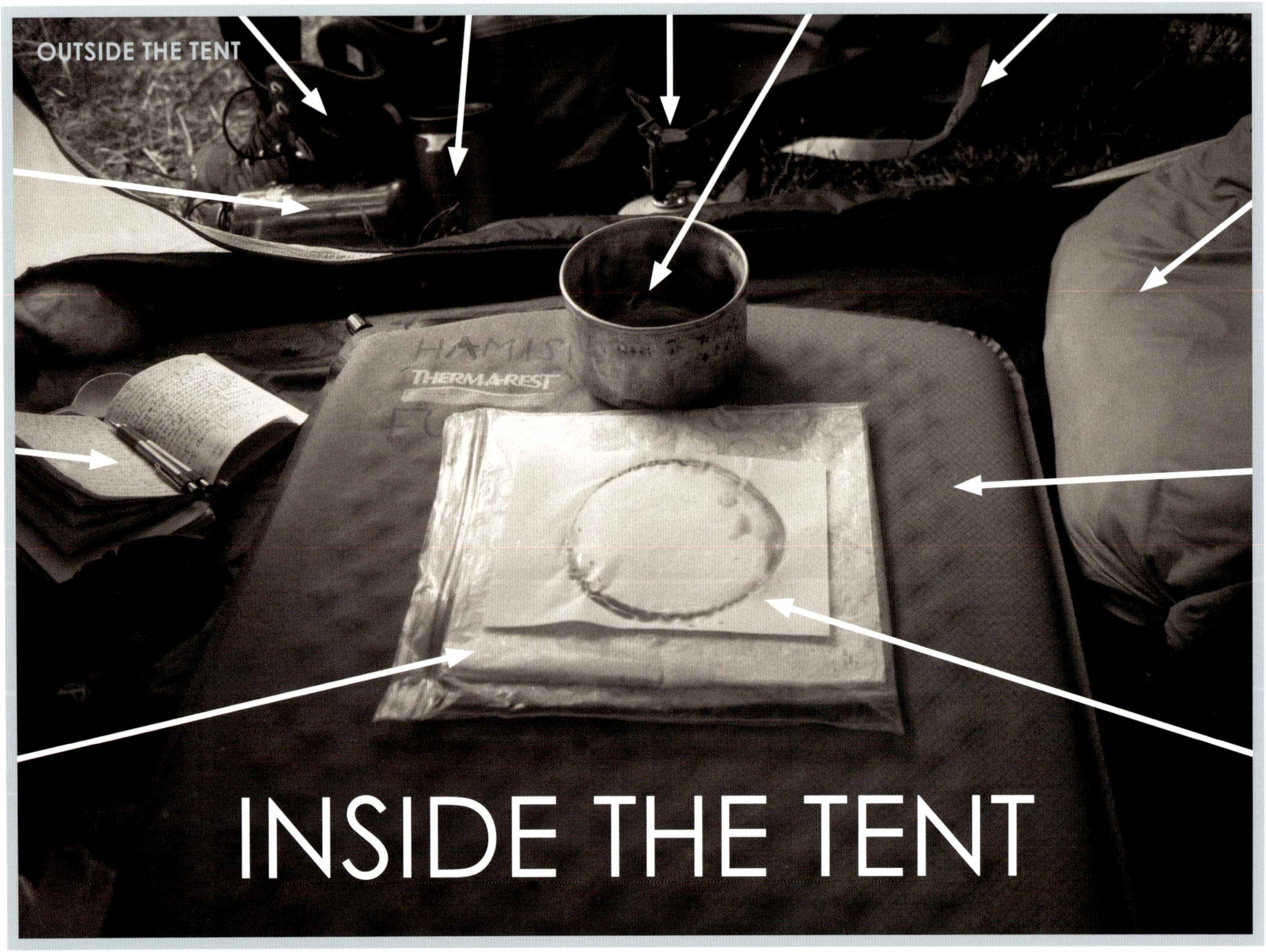

Nalgene bottle.

2010 walk diary and pens.

Cairngorms map inside Ziplock bag.

Waterproof sack used as pillow containing clothes and Arcteryx Alpha SV Goretex jacket

Inflatable Thermarest.

Tentart—outline of the cooking pot.

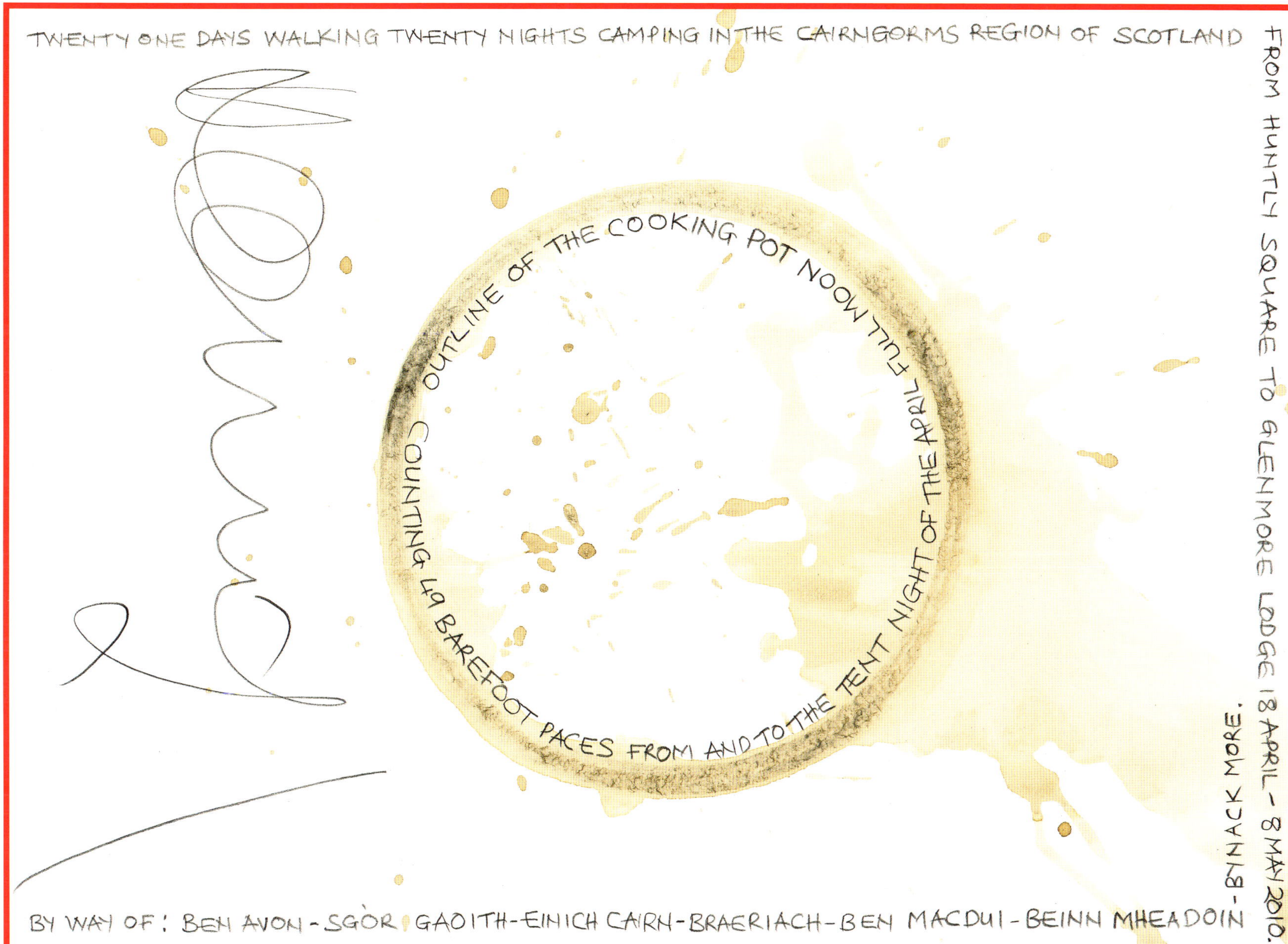

Hamish Fulton. Outline of the Cooking Pot. Coffee ring and pencil text on paper. 2010

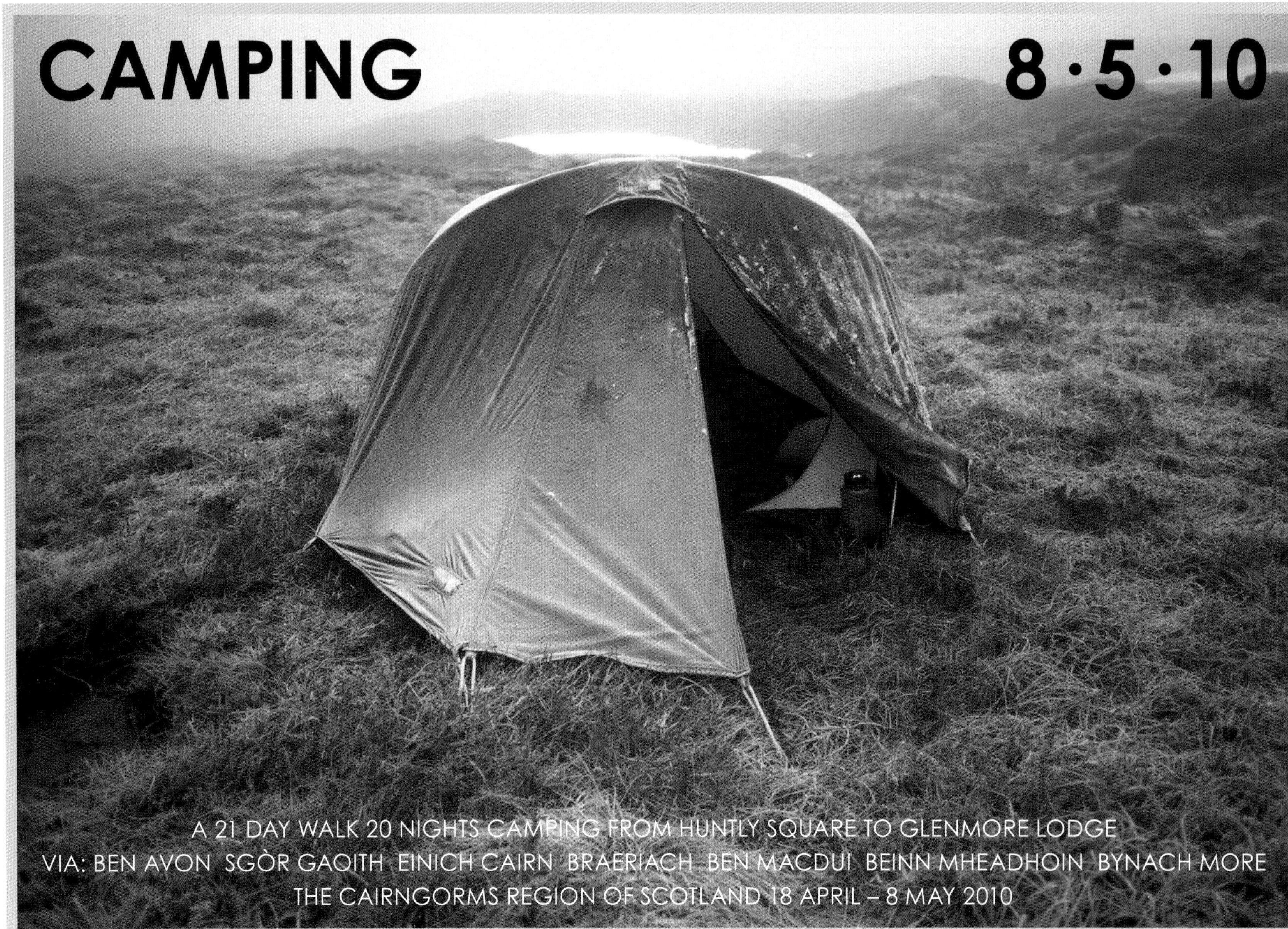
CAMPING
8·5·10
A 21 DAY WALK 20 NIGHTS CAMPING FROM HUNTLY SQUARE TO GLENMORE LODGE
VIA: BEN AVON SGÒR GAOITH EINICH CAIRN BRAERIACH BEN MACDUI BEINN MHEADHOIN BYNACH MORE
THE CAIRNGORMS REGION OF SCOTLAND 18 APRIL – 8 MAY 2010

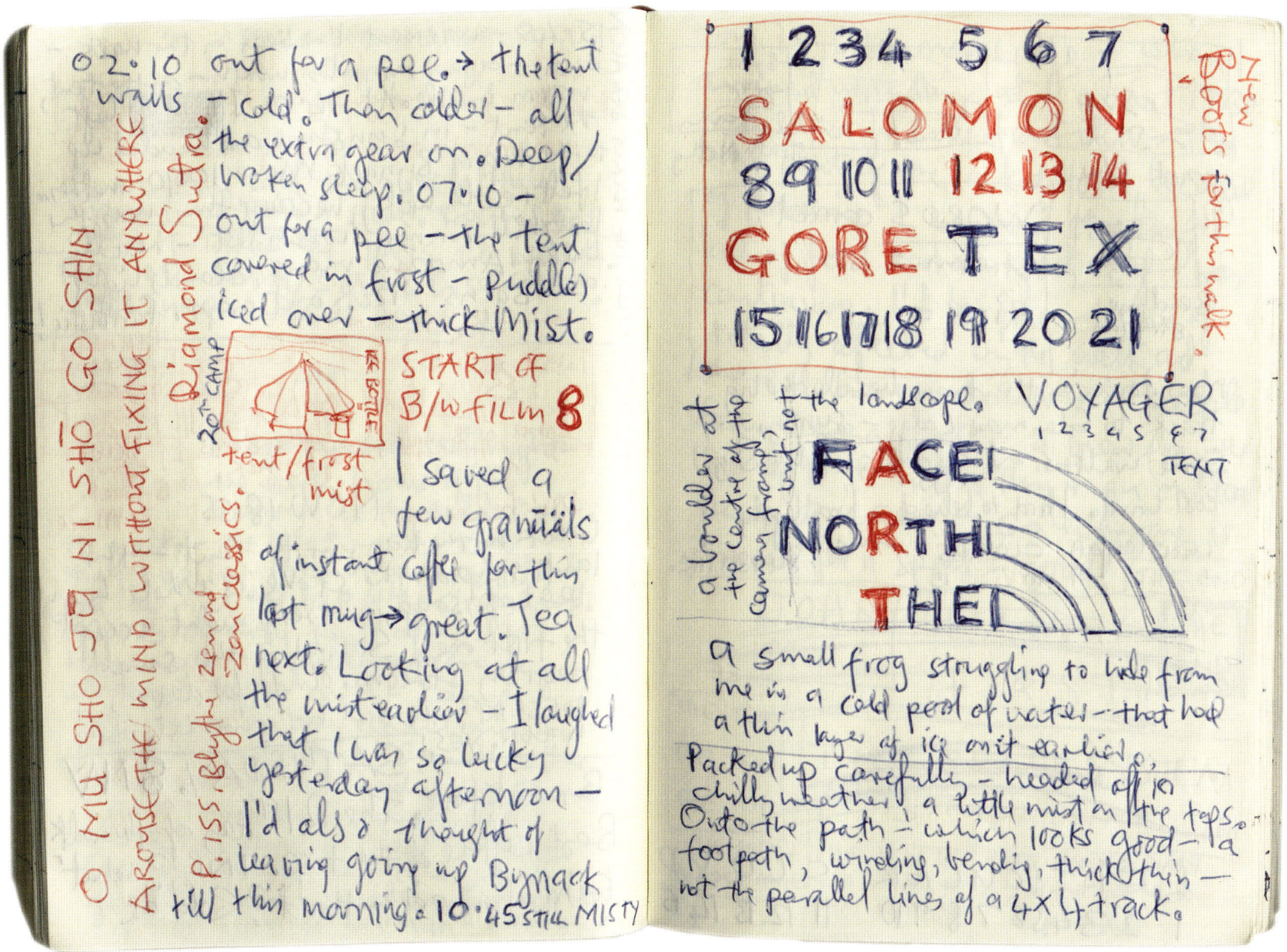
02.10 out for a pee. → the tent walls – cold. Then colder – all the extra gear on. Deep/broken sleep. 07.10 – out for a pee – the tent covered in frost – puddles iced over – thick Mist.

20th CAMP
ICE BOTTLE
tent/frost mist

START OF B/W FILM 8

I saved a few granuals of instant coffee for this last mug → great. Tea next. Looking at all the mist earlier – I laughed that I was so lucky yesterday afternoon – I'd also thought of leaving going up Bynack till this morning. 10.45 STILL MISTY

O MU SHO JU NI SHO GO SHIN
AROUSE THE MIND WITHOUT FIXING IT ANYWHERE
Diamond Sutra.
P. 155, Blyth Zen and Zen Classics.

1 2 3 4 5 6 7
SALOMON
8 9 10 11 12 13 14
GORE TEX
15 16 17 18 19 20 21

New Boots for this walk.

a boulder at the centre of the camera frame, but not the landscape.

VOYAGER
1 2 3 4 5 6 7
TENT

FACE
NORTH
THE

A small frog struggling to hide from me in a cold pool of water – that had a thin layer of ice on it earlier.

Packed up carefully – headed off in chilly weather, a little mist on the tops. Onto the path – which looks good – a footpath, winding, bending, thick thin – not the parallel lines of a 4x4 track.

Hamish Fulton. Cairngorms Diary, Spring 2010

1 2 3 4 5 6 7

A 21 DAY WALK 20 NIGHTS CAMPING

S A L O M O N

FROM HUNTLY SQUARE TO GLENMORE LODGE

8 9 10 11 12 13 14

VIA: BEN AVON SGÒR GAOITH EINICH CAIRN BRAERIACH BEN MACDUI BEINN MHEADHOIN BYNACH MORE

G O R E T E X

THE CAIRNGORMS REGION OF SCOTLAND 18 APRIL – 8 MAY 2010

15 16 17 18 19 20 21

WILD CITY. (The rock is in the centre of the camera frame, but not the landscape.) Design as decoy. The so-called titles of my text works are purposely 'built' with words having the same number of letters as the days walked. (See pages 5, 8, 10, 31, 48, 65, 76.) The 'title' phrases or single words are intended to complement or contradict the walk – either way they expand the topic and increase the interconnections. This system 'locks' the graphic layout of the walk text. **IT'S WHAT THE ART IS ABOUT – NOT WHAT IT LOOKS LIKE.** (Irrespective of its appearance, contemporary art is a necessary political force in society.) Stillness. Lying on my back in the sleeping bag, watching a small insect move in and out of the 5mm squares of tent fabric. No skim reading, no speed reading in the tent. Wild camping slowness, time to read and re-read haiku poems. Time to concentrate. Respect the Mountain (see page 6), this photograph of my tent was 'taken' in the Swiss Alps – where camping is not normal or advised. (During a blizzard the following morning this particular tent was blown away.) At my exhibition in Courmayeur, I had an interesting conversation with Giovanni from Chamonix. He pointed out to me that my artwork about summiting Mont Blanc (2009) was not a true ascent – since I was guided – since I had bowed to convention – taken a cable car and spent the night at Refuge Des Cosmiques (but descended via Grande Bosse)**!** I also learnt that Chamonix, capital of alpinism, does not have a contemporary art space. Climbers, it seems, prefer representational art. Camping for 20 nights in the Cairngorms was an experience of both reduction and accumulation. No alcohol, no sound pollution, and a big reduction of food intake. Drinking from mountains. Drinking clean water directly from streams (Gaelic: abhainn = river, allt = burn; Scots for a small stream). Once, I remember walking uphill feeling weak from the lack of food. Eventually, I adjusted to the physical routine which was not so difficult but the benefits were profound. Clarity and accumulating calmness. All, under the influence of nature. *When the time is right*, more balance, more happiness. Although the balance faded, it left an impression. Retreat – is a seven-letter word. Visitor – is a seven letter word. I was a visitor to the hills. From a train to a train. I also noted in my diary that: Deer run away, ptarmigan fly away, mountain hares race away, frogs submerge in pools – away from my human presence. I saw two categories of unwanted human traces inside the Cairngorms. Unofficial marks by people using saws to cut down branches to build shelters and fires – fires inside stone rings. *It's harder to leave things alone than to change them*. There would not be such a big ideological leap from this 'woodcraft' habit to *leave no trace*. (Tent and stove.) The second human mark is the 'official' mark, the bulldozed road that Jim Crumley mentions. A good example in 2010 can be found in GLEANN EINICH. ***Park your car ride a bike, stash your bike take a hike.*** Opinion – is a seven letter word. **A WALK IS A FACT FOR THE WALKER AND FICTION FOR EVERYONE ELSE. A WALK CAN EXIST LIKE AN INVISIBLE OBJECT IN A COMPLEX WORLD. A STRONG IDEA CAN GENERATE AND SUSTAIN PHYSICAL ENERGY. EACH WALK MARKS THE FLOW OF TIME BETWEEN BIRTH AND DEATH. ALL MY WALKS ARE RELATED FROM THE FIRST TO THE LAST.** ***MAKE A WALK WRITE A TEXT READ IT TO AN AUDIENCE.***

In 2000, while wandering through a bookstore, this time in Edinburgh, my eye was caught by the title *A High and Lonely Place*. On page 120, the author Jim Crumley writes:
"A hundred-year government commitment to the restoration of the Cairngorms wilderness. A hundred years is the figure Adam Watson has used to indicate how long the worst damage would take to heal, but it is an arbitrary number which may prove to be too short. We have no serious government involvement in the welfare of wild landscape, a fact which is itself a serious charge to lay against any European nation. 'Restoration wilderness' would imply the dismantling of every man-made artefact in the mountains, all skiing developments, all roads, car parks, building, bulldozed roads, even bothies and bridges, allied to a determined programme of restoration on the ground. It also implies relieving the pressure of people on the ground, if not by physical exclusion then certainly by denying people artificially easy forms of access. Cairn Gorm would quickly begin to recover, for example, if the nearest car park was at Coylumbridge."
This paragraph was and is a great inspiration to me. My thanks to Jim Crumley for agreeing to contribute to this Charta publication. His words speak of a lifelong deep affection for the Cairngorms.

Wild – An Elemental Journey (2006) by Jay Griffiths (taking seven years to complete) is a book I return to, a reference point. In 2010, the existence of the wild is of the greatest importance, there is nothing more important. From the wild, everything flows. My thanks to Jay Griffiths.

For the opportunity to assemble this book my thanks go to Claudia Zeiske, director of Deveron Arts. Claudia organised the funding for this project, arranged the group walks, introduced me to Mary Jane Jacob and contacted my two best choice authors.

My thanks to Giuseppe Liverani for this my third book with Charta.

Special thanks to:
Anna, Nick, Norma, Tony.
Simon Fildes
Timothy Brennan (two seven-letter names)
Michael Setek
Colin Sackett
Casey Fulton

Hamish Fulton, August 2010

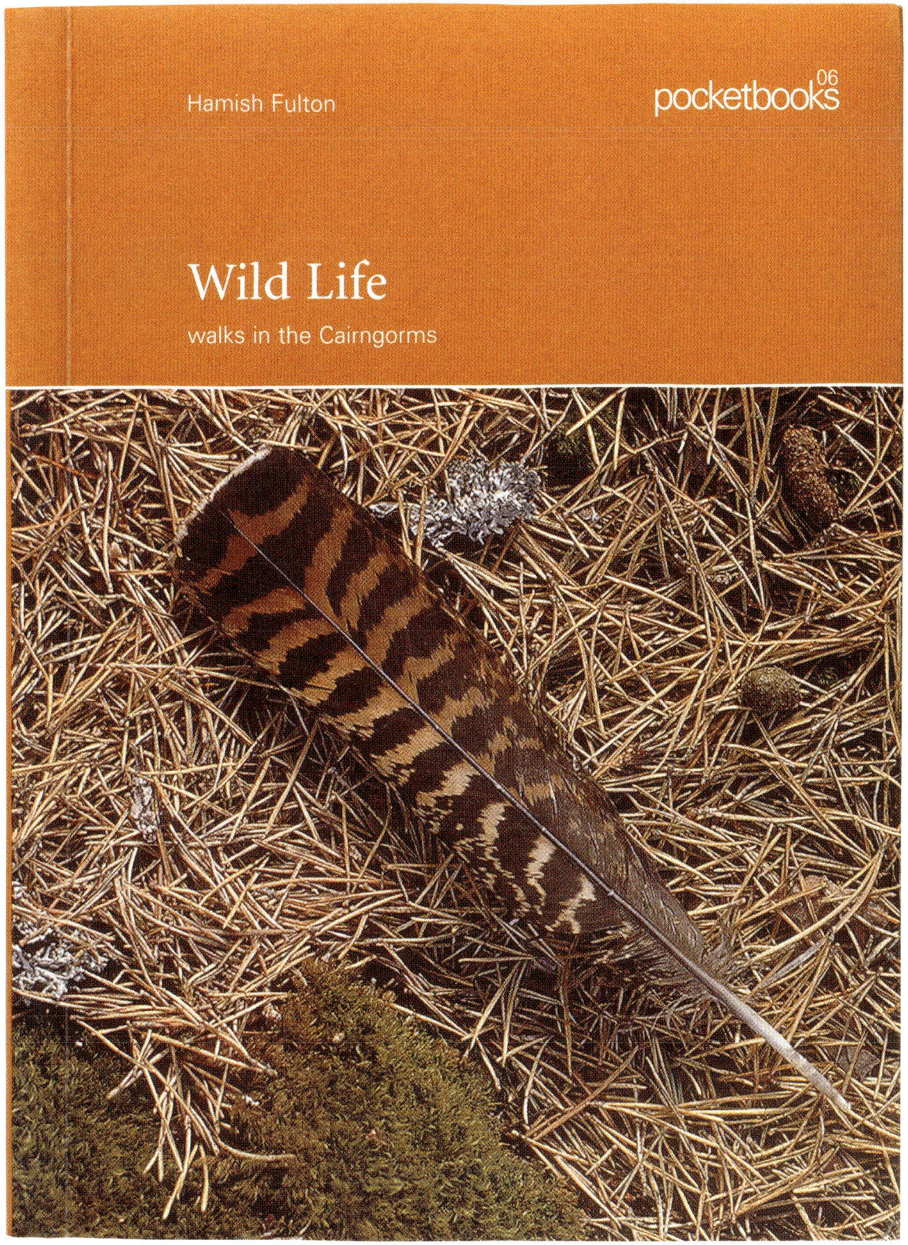

HAMISH FULTON
Selection of recent artists books – by region

2010 *The Uncarved Block* – Himalayas
Lars Müller Publishers
2008 *El Camino* – Iberian Peninsula
Fundación Ortega Muñoz
2006 *Geronimo Homeland* – Gila Wilderness
Texas Gallery / Christine Burgin
2000 *Magpie* – Canadian Prairie
Southern Alberta Art Gallery
Wild Life – Cairngorms, Scotland
Pocketbooks, Edinburgh
Higurashi – Japan
C.C.A. Kitakyushu

HAMISH FULTON
Selected overview publications

2005 *Keep Moving*
Museion Bolzano / Charta,
Exhibition Catalogue
2002 *Walking Journey*
Tate Publishing, Exhibition Catalogue
2001 *Walking Artist*
Richter Verlag

Design Hamish Fulton
Layout Colin Sackett
Editorial Coordination Daniela Meda, Filomena Moscatelli
Copyediting Charles Gute
Copywriting and Press Office Silvia Palombi
US Editorial Director Francesca Sorace
Promotion and Web Monica D'Emidio
Distribution Antonia De Besi
Administration Grazia De Giosa
Warehouse and Outlet Roberto Curiale

Cover design The artist
Photo Credits Unless otherwise stated, by the artist.

ISBN 978-88-8158-791-9
Printed in October 2010
by BIANCA&VOLTA, Truccazzano, Italy

Edizioni Charta srl
Milano
via della Moscova, 27-20121
Tel. +39-026598098/026598200
Fax +39-026598577
e-mail: charta@chartaartbooks.it

Charta Books Ltd.
New York City
Tel. +1-313-406-8468
e-mail: international@chartaartbooks.it
www.chartaartbooks.it

This book was commissioned by Deveron Arts / the town is the venue: www.deveron-arts.com

THIS PROJECT HAS BEEN PART-FINANCED BY THE CAIRNGORMS NATIONAL PARK AUTHORITY, THE SCOTTISH GOVERNMENT AND THE EUROPEAN COMMUNITY
Cairngorms Local Action Group LEADER 2007 – 2013 Programme